Let him who has ears to hear

hear the story of a life that was headed in the wrong direction.

Then Jesus came in and turned it in the right direction.

Other Books By The Happy Hunters

Angels On Assignment
Are You Tired?
Born Again! What Do You Mean?
Come Alive
Follow Me
Go, Man, Go
God's Answer To Fat...LOØSE IT!
God's Conditions For Prosperity
Handbook For Healing
Hang Loose With Jesus
Heart To Heart Flip Chart
His Power Through You
Holy Laughter
How Do You Treat My Son Jesus?
How To Heal The Sick
How To Make Your Marriage Exciting
How To Pick A Perfect Husband...Or Wife
How To Receive & Maintain A Healing
How To Receive & Minister The Baptism With The Holy Spirit
I Don't Follow Signs & Wonders...They Follow Me
If Charles & Frances Can Do It, YOU Can Do It, Too!
If You Really Love Me...
Impossible Miracles
Let This Mind Be In You
Memorizing Made Easy
P.T.L.A. (Praise The Lord Anyway)
Since Jesus Passed By
the fabulous Skinnie Minnie Recipe Book
Strength For Today
Supernatural Horizons (From Glory To Glory)
The Two Sides Of A Coin
There Are Two Kinds Of...
This Way Up!
Video Study Guide-How To Heal The Sick (15 Hours)
Video Study Guide-How To Heal The Sick Power Pack (6 Hours)

God Is Fabulous revised edition
ISBN 1-878209-15-9

Scriptures quoted from The New King James Version, Thomas Nelson Publishers, Nashville, Tennessee, unless otherwise noted.
Authorized King James Version (KJV)

God Is Fabulous, original edition, ISBN 0-87162-115-0

God Is Fabulous 30th Anniversary Edition

A Note From
Frances Gardner Hunter...

When I wrote "God Is Fabulous," the world was a different place. Now it seems everything has changed: cars, computers, televisions, life in general. Even my name has changed since then! The one thing that hasn't changed, though, is the excitement I felt as I first sat down to write this book thirty years ago.

Every time I read this little book, my heart is filled with the joy and overflowing peace that Jesus brought into my life, just like that first day I met Him. I know that you will have the same reaction when you read it for the first time or the twentieth.

I meet many people who tell me that the thrill of serving Jesus is just not like it was when they first were born again. It's my belief and my prayer that when you open the pages of this book, Jesus will fill you up with the same excitement and anticipation you experienced when you first asked Him into your heart, and that you will once again remember the fact that truly...

God Is Fabulous!

Dedicated To
"The Men In My Life"

Jesus Christ, without whom this book could never have been lived or written;

Rev. H. Peter Slagle, who heard my soul cry out, and who lovingly led me to Jesus;

Ed Waxer, Area Director for the Campus Crusade for Christ, to whom I am a debtor because of the time he took in helping me learn how to win others to Jesus;

Rick Strawbridge, another outstanding member of Campus Crusade for Christ, for the "young" viewpoint he gave me of Christianity; and

Gene Cotton, folk singer, who in blind faith joined with me in a vision.

Frances Gardner Hunter

Foreword

Frances Gardner is the type of Christian who if asked to pray for rain would carry an umbrella to her place of prayer. Her endless enthusiasm and immovable faith keep her ready for immediate action for the sake of Jesus Christ.

The effervescence of her personality, her refreshing honesty, and her ability to deal directly from the level of human interest, has enabled this Christian writer to prepare a book applicable to scores of people floundering in a faulty faith. The style of writing is fresh and entertaining and strikes where people act and react. The chapter on prayer is a typical example of her distinctive style. It is both amusing and enlightening.

In my work as the Crusade Director for the citywide and area-wide crusades of the Ford Philpot Evangelistic Association, I am constantly searching for people alive with the spirit of evangelism. Frances Gardner has proved to be such a one. In our preparation for the South Miami Crusade, she labored diligently to assist our efforts. God is using her written and personal witness to win countless souls to her "fabulous" Savior.

We of the Ford Philpot Evangelistic Association have appreciated her support and friendship, and it is with unmasked confidence that we predict beneficial inspiration for all who read the pages of this book.

Jimmy Sowder

Table Of Contents

Chapter 1

I Meet Jesus Christ

"I have come that they may have life, and that they may have it more abundantly" (John 10:10).

"For all have sinned and fall short of the glory of God" (Romans 3:23).

"For by grace you have been saved through faith, and that not of yourselves; it is the gift of God, not of works, lest anyone should boast" (Ephesians 2:8-9).

Three very short verses of Scripture, but three very important verses in my personal encounter with Jesus Christ. It is my prayer that God will allow these three verses to be very important in your life, too. Important because of what they can do for you.

I'd like to share with you how I met Jesus Christ personally. And my only reason for writing this book is a prayer that it will reach the millions of people who are **"unsaved" Christians** like I was. My prayer is that something in this book will come across to YOU in such a way that you will look at your own life in an honest appraisal of how you stand with Jesus Christ. I sincerely wish I had made an appraisal of myself earlier in life.

I had been a "Christian" all my life. I was raised in a church, went to church for many years, helped make the great decisions of Christianity such as "Do we have tuna fish or creamed cheese for sandwiches," but it took me forty-eight years of life to discover **"how to get the most out of life after *most* of life was gone."**

Don't let this happen to you!

As I look back now, I can see that God spoke to me many times in my life, but for many years my hardheaded self-approved ability to do things myself made me buck His wonderful outstretched arms without realizing that what I was doing is probably the biggest prevailing sin in the world today – the sin of ignoring God and of compromising with Christianity – or putting it off until tomorrow because of "not being ready."

I Just Drifted

I had drifted away from church during the last ten years because, as I told every minister who came into my office, I could be just as good a Christian outside of church as I could be *inside*. You can, but you won't! Church honestly bored me, and my most awful thoughts came to me while sitting in church. Obviously I wasn't listening in spite of my so-called Christianity, so I began to find excuses for not attending church. After a few years I didn't even find it necessary to make excuses.

Everyone just accepted the fact (so I thought) that I was a mighty Christian without going to church. And, anyway, after working eighteen to twenty hours a day for six days, I was entitled to sleep on Sunday, wasn't I? After all, I did have to make a living to support my children, didn't I?

The Bible says: *"You shall have no other gods before Me."* Well, I never did. You wouldn't either, would you? Like the god of money...the god of excitement...the god of cocktails before dinner...the god of cigarettes...the god of dancing sexy, stimulating dances for the physical thrill it gives...the god of clothes...the god of dirty jokes...the god of swear words just to show people you're "cool"...Did you ever place any of these "gods" first in your life? Well, I'm glad you didn't, because I DID! And because I was compromising with Christianity I still went along in my little ivory palace with a slightly tarnished halo around my head.

But God has an interesting way of dealing with people like me. I shall always feel that God loved me very much because He really went out of His way to bring me into His fold. I wonder if any maverick was ever broken who kicked as hard and as long as I did.

My only son was married in 1965, and shortly before his marriage I was in an automobile accident. Little did I realize what would result from this, but three months after the accident I made the horrible discovery that I had lost the sight of my left eye.

You may think this is an awful tragedy, but I consider it the greatest blessing of my life – it took a tragedy like this to bring me to a realization of what *I didn't have in life.*

Quite accidentally at two o'clock in the morning on a Saturday night I discovered that I could not see out of my left eye. This was a tremendous shock. I had been out for dinner and cocktails with a friend, and had started to read before I went to bed. Although I had my glasses on, I suddenly realized I couldn't see.

I was dumbfounded, but when I put my hand up to my glasses I found that the lens of the right glass had popped out. I reached into my evening bag and, sure enough, there it was! I replaced it in the frame and started reading. About twenty minutes later the startling thought struck me, "Only the right lens popped out – how come I couldn't see *anything?*"

Something prompted me to shut the right eye and hold it with my finger (I never could wink that eye), and to my horror I discovered that the left eye was without vision.

I promptly decided I had had too much to drink and, like Scarlet O'Hara, thought, I'll worry about that tomorrow. Tomorrow came bright and early and with it the recollection that I had had only one drink, and that I had driven home. So I made the same one eye test I had tried the night before, and it confirmed the truth I'd tried to avoid.

I couldn't see!

On Sunday I didn't know where to reach an ophthalmologist, so I called my optometrist and told him I couldn't see. He told me to drop by and see him the next morning on my way to work. I don't believe there has ever been a day as horrible for me as Sunday, May 16, 1965. I read medical articles in every encyclopedia I could lay my hands on and before the day was over I knew I had a cataract of some kind.

That day was the birthday of the husband of a friend of mine, and I had a party for him. How I lived through it I don't know. I was smiling on the outside, but on the inside I was dying. Little did I know it then, but I actually was dying – because I think this is the event that triggered my dying to self. God was really working in my life.

During the four and a half years which preceded this accident, a certain minister had been bringing printing jobs into my office, and while I enjoyed his conversation immensely, I was deaf to his entreaties about Christianity and attending church. Still, I developed a tremendous liking for him and his theories even though I didn't practice them.

There was one thing he did, though, that didn't set right with me. He always talked about the "Lord," and I asked him one day why he didn't say "God" instead of the "Lord." I didn't tell him so, but I really thought he sounded kinda "kooky" talking about his "Lord." Even though he was a young minister, I thought he was probably some kind of an old-fashioned fuddy-duddy.

God Closed In

I bring in the fact that a particular minister prayed

for me for four and a half years at this time because God was really closing in on me, even though I didn't know it.

I went to the optometrist before I opened my office the next morning and told no one what I suspected (because "I" could always handle every situation), but I did tell my head girl that I had a little eye problem.

It was several hours before I returned to the office, and everyone knew that something had happened.

And something had!

The initial examination revealed the horrible truth that a cataract had covered the lens of my eye. The optometrist took me to an ophthalmologist who said surgery was necessary. (I had already started having blinding headaches.)

Because I was so all powerful, I said "Let's get it over with, when can I go in?" This was on Monday, and I was scheduled for surgery on Friday morning.

The surgeon told me that they would remove the lens of the eye and that for four to six months I would have the eye patched, and then a contact and glasses would allow 20/20 vision.

I cried.

Because my two children have been raised without a father, I have not allowed myself the luxury of crying very often. A mother alone has to be strong. I asked the doctor if he would allow me the privilege of being completely feminine for a few minutes and then I'd be all right.

I cried.

And I cried real hard.

I returned to my office after asking God to take good care of me, and bluntly announced what had happened. The young minister who always talked about his "Lord" was there by coincidence or was God working in my life?

Because I was struggling for composure, I announced that the girls could quit crying on my time since I was paying them. Then I said to the young minister, "They probably think you'll be the first one at my bedside when I come back from surgery." Now why he should be at my bedside when I had never darkened the doors of his church, and had repeatedly told him I didn't need to go to church, I'll never know – or do I?

I made all the frantic preparations necessary before going to the hospital; I was due to arrive at five o'clock on Thursday night, May 20, but I didn't get there until seven o'clock!

There has been placed in every human being a God-shaped vacuum. Until we have filled that God-shaped vacuum with a personal relationship with the Lord Jesus Christ, we do a lot of other things to try to fill the vacuum. Nestled deeply and firmly in our hearts God has placed eternity and nothing will ever satisfy us until we fill that vacuum with Him.

About a quarter to five all of my brave thoughts had drained right out of my toes. My God-shaped vacuum began getting bigger and bigger. Since a martini was the only antidote for fear that I knew of, I began downing one after another. I wouldn't admit to anybody that I was scared, but in my heart I was absolutely petrified! The doctor had explained all the gory details of the operation, which is very simple today, but it wasn't at that time. None of this appealed to me one single solitary bit.

I continued to down martinis and light one cigarette after another. I finally got to the hospital two hours late with much too much to drink! Unfortunately, at that time this was the only way I knew to try to fill that God-shaped vacuum. How I praise God and give Him my everlasting thanks that the void and the vacuum are filled today!

Dusting Off My Bible

Because I was such a devout "Christian" in times of crisis, I was shocked to discover that my maid had not put my Bible in my suitcase, and I knew I couldn't possibly undergo surgery without my "precious" Bible!

I called the friend whose husband had the birthday the Sunday before and asked her to run over to my house and bring my Bible, because she understood I simply couldn't go to surgery without reading my precious Bible. She asked, "Where is it?"

I said, "Look in the back bedroom on the top shelf of the closet, way in the back, and you'll find my Bible which I love so much – it's the one dated 1924 – be sure and dust it off (I hadn't read it since my last operation) and bring it to me quickly." After all, what do we all do in a crisis? We really call on God in a hurry, don't we? Maybe you don't, but I always did. I have never known anybody who went to the hospital and called out, "Devil! Help me!"

Very shortly she was there with my Bible which I opened to Psalm 23 because that was the only thing I had ever read in the Bible up to that time.

I called the nurses in to make sure that they knew what a great saint they had on their hands. I read that verse very, very dramatically, *"The Lord is my shepherd; I shall not want."*

I closed the Bible.

I "religiously" thought I was spiritually prepared for whatever happened next. You may ask, "Why did you only read one verse?" When I had my gall bladder taken out, the operation lasted 4 1/2 to 5 hours. I had read all six verses of the 23rd Psalm for that surgery. The eye operation would just take about thirty minutes so in my little sinner's mind I figured out that all I had to do was read one verse for a thirty-minute operation.

As I closed the Bible I thought, "I'll give God a break. I'll pray." Even though I was 48 years of age I did not know how to pray. I could say the Lord's Prayer backwards and forwards but I honestly didn't know how to pray. Real praying is when your heart cries out to God for a very vital need in your life.

I continued, "I guess I can order God around just like I order people in my printing company." I looked up and shook my finger at the ceiling of that hospital room as I said, "God, don't let it hurt! After it's over, then You can let it hurt...a little bit." I stopped for a second and thought, "Maybe I was being too severe," so I continued, "but please don't let it hurt while the operation is going on. Thank you very much."

With that I laid back on the pillow. I had been so "spiritual" and so "religious," I was sure that the glowing light from my tremendous halo streamed underneath the door of the room and radiated into the corridors of the hospital.

As I relaxed with my counterfeit glowing halo, I was suddenly jolted into reality and thought, "What did that say?" I remembered that I knew only two verses of scripture by memory and Psalm 23:1 was one of them and I hadn't really read it. I reached over and grabbed my Bible. I opened it to the 23rd Psalm.

Nothing was there!

The page which had the 23rd Psalm printed on it a few minutes ago, was totally blank! Now there was *nothing* on those pages. There was no printing, no words, no nothing! It was snow white!

I was in the printing business. One thing I knew was, once ink is laid down on a piece of paper, it is impossible to remove!

God had done a miracle!

God had supernaturally wiped all the ink off the page. God had spoken to me in a way I could easily understand.

As I stared at the white blank page where the 23rd Psalm should have been, I suddenly saw something I will never forget because it is indelibly burned on my heart.

I saw the finger of God descending from heaven and I saw Him begin to write where the 23rd Psalm had been. The words were written in the brightest red I've ever seen. **God had dipped His finger in the brilliant red blood of Jesus and had written a very special message just for me.** *"Frances Gardner"* (that was my name then) was on the left hand side and on the right hand side He wrote, *"I love you."*

Of all the people in the world God said He loved *me*.

I think in one world-shattering moment I got a glimpse of what my life had been – a constant, "Oh, God, *YOU* do this for me!" And never a thought as to what I could do for Him.

I didn't know what I was doing really, but in that moment I said, "God, I take back that prayer, and I don't care how much it hurts tomorrow, I promise You this: when I get out of this hospital, **I will spend the rest of my life seeing what I can do for You, and not what You can do for me."**

Little do we realize what we say in times like this, and how much truth is spoken during trials and tribulations.

As a drunken sinner in a hospital bed, I had said the secret of the Christian life – not what God can do for you but what you can do for God!

There are many promises made on a hospital bed and unfortunately there are more promises broken when people walk out of the hospital door than any place else but this was one thing I meant.

I wasn't sure who God was, I was still in shock. One thing I knew without a doubt in my heart, though, was that God loved Frances Gardner.

19

I wasn't alone any more!

I returned from surgery the next morning at about eleven, and there, standing by my bed, was the young minister who served his "Lord." I was so doped up I didn't make much sense, but one sentence came out. "The first place I'm going when I get out of the hospital is to your church!" I'll never forget the funny smile that came on his face!

God knew that one of His sheep was lost and He had sent a shepherd to find her and lovingly bring her into the fold.

My recovery was excellent, and in just ten days I returned to work wearing all sorts of fancy eye patches. I had one for every dress I owned. Even though I wore a broad smile on the outside, I had discovered that something was missing from my life. This kind of an operation destroys your depth perception. I couldn't drive my car. I couldn't get my food into my mouth without spilling it all over me. It can be a frustrating time with a patch over your eye twenty-four hours a day!

Going To Church

But I remembered what I had promised God in the hospital, and before my operation was two weeks old, I went to church. I was so weak I could hardly make it, but somewhere God had given me a taste of the living water and it started a compelling desire for MORE. . . MORE. . . MORE!

Communion was served that day and when communion was finished, the pastor stood up and said, "Normally I don't preach after communion, but today I feel 'led' to give a sermon."

I looked around the church and thought, "I don't see anybody leading him. I wonder what he means." Today I know. The Holy Spirit had said to him, "You have a red hot sinner in here, don't let her out!" And he didn't!

He didn't have a sermon prepared so he opened his Bible and read the most peculiar words I ever heard, *"There was a man of the Pharisees named Nicodemus, a ruler of the Jews. This man came to Jesus by night and said to Him, 'Rabbi, we know that You are a teacher come from God: for no one can do these signs that You do unless God is with him.'*

"Jesus answered and said to him, 'Most assuredly, I say to you, unless one is born again, he cannot see the kingdom of God.'" (John 3:1-3)

I thought, "Born again? My mother is dead. My mother has been dead for years. How can I possibly be born again?"

I never felt so miserable in my whole life! I was glad he kept on reading because Nicodemus apparently had the same problem that I did. However, I felt like the pastor was reading my mind instead of the Bible.

"Nicodemus said to Him, 'How can a man be born when he is old? Can he enter a second time into his mother's womb and be born?'

"Jesus answered, 'Most assuredly, I say to you, unless one is born of water and the Spirit, he cannot

enter the kingdom of God. That which is born of the flesh is flesh, and that which is born of the Spirit is spirit. Do not marvel that I said to you, You must be born again.'"

In that one split second, I knew something that I had never known before. I knew for certain that I wasn't "born again." I felt awful. I had no idea how to *get* born again or *be* born again or *find* born again!

My first thought was: "I certainly can't tell God. God thinks I'm a Christian. After all those years that I've gone to church, God thinks I'm a Christian. I can't let God know that I'm not."

My first inclination was to go home and hide under the bed so even God couldn't find me or see me. In my heart I knew that I had never been born again. I knew that I had not really been a Christian.

I was so shaken up that Sunday, I didn't even listen completely. But he did say something about Jesus standing at the door of my heart, knocking, and asking me to open the door. He continued with something about asking for forgiveness of my sins.

"Well," I thought, "that bit about the forgiveness of sins was about the most stupid thing I ever heard. I am absolutely without sin. After all, wasn't I donating printing jobs to churches? And wasn't I being a real good little 'do bee'? And don't forget the tuna fish sandwiches I made for the church suppers."

The Bible says, *"All have sinned and fall short of the glory of God."*

"It does?" I wondered, "I don't remember hearing that before. After all those years of sitting in those other churches, all I remember is something about Moses floating down a river."

The pastor stopped talking.

Then he did something I had never seen before: he made an altar call! I had never been in a church where people sang at the end of the service.

They began to sing, "Just As I Am." I think every sinner has heard that song, so I thought I would join in. I sang only four words, "Just as I am." I burst into tears. Not just "regular" tears, but real soul-searching tears! I boo-hooed and I boo-hooed.

I couldn't stop crying!

The music went on and on and on and on. They sang, "Just As I Am" three times, five times, ten times, twenty times, fifty-seven times!

"This is a miserable church!" I thought. "Won't they ever stop?" I couldn't stop crying. It was violent sobbing which shook my very being from my head to my toes. I did not have a tissue in my pocket or my pocketbook. My nose was dripping, my eyes were running, my makeup was a mess!

What an encounter! For the first time in my life **I realized I was *not* a Christian.** I certainly didn't admit it to anyone – not even myself! What a horrible discovery to make when you're forty-eight years old. I remember thinking, I can't let God know about this, because He thinks I'm a Christian. Oh, foolish woman, God knew it all the time. I was so confused and in such a state of shock to even *think* that I might not be a Christian, that I didn't know what to do.

Finally it was over! I ran out to my car as I lit a

cigarette. I blew smoke all over that church and said vehemently, "I'll never come back to this dumb church again. Never! Never! Never! I want a church that makes me feel good! I don't need a church that makes me feel miserable."

Guess where I was the next Sunday morning? I was right back in that same little church! God had lovingly placed one drop of the living water of life upon my thirsty tongue, and once you've tasted the precious living water of life, nothing else will satisfy. I had no choice except to go back to the same little church. But I was prepared this time: I had six Kleenex with me!

The pastor was most unusual because he had done something during the week that I could not believe. He had visited all my personal friends and had asked them all about me – and they told him everything they knew so he proceeded to tell the entire congregation during the church service.

Every word he spoke was directed at me, just me. Everything pointed at my life and me.

"For all have sinned and fall short of the glory of God."

"Not me," I thought. "God, remember the tuna fish sandwiches? Remember the cream cheese sandwiches? Remember all the dishes I washed after the church suppers?" This was before the day of dishwashers, and I would sing "I'm working my way to heaven, to heaven, to heaven…" as I stacked the dishes higher and higher!

The pastor continued to read, *"Thou shalt place no other gods before me."*

Our money says, 'In God We Trust.' I thought, "I trust my money so that means I trust God. I've never been to a church where they did or said these kinds of things." I didn't like it.

"Thou shalt place no other gods before me," he repeated. "What do you put first in your life? Cigarettes?"

I thought, "I don't like you." I felt as if his finger was pointing directly at me.

"Martinis?" Yes! His finger was pointing at me!

"FUN?" His finger was getting longer and more pointed! Whatever he said and wherever his finger went, he pointed directly at me!

With an artificial grin on my face, I thought "I hate you! I'll never come back to this dumb church as long as I live!"

Then they started that song again! I lost my composure completely and burst into tears as they rose from the pews and starting singing "Just As I Am."

I ran out of the church.

As I got outside and caught my breath, I stomped my feet again and said, "I hate this church. I'll never come back! I'll never come back. I'll never come back." I lit up a cigarette and blew smoke all over the church as I continued to carry on. "I'll never come back to this dumb church again!" I jumped into my car, gunned the motor and scratched out of the parking lot, throwing gravel all over the place.

When I reached the haven of my own home, the first thing I did was to make myself a martini so I would feel better. Then I had another one and I felt a little better.

The church where I had previously "visited" once or twice a year seemed safe enough. They didn't do any of those strange things. They never made me cry. I was going back there.

The following Sunday, I got in my car and drove over to my "safe, comfortable" church. I drove into the parking lot, and suddenly my car turned right around! I drove down the street and turned into the parking lot of that junky old church!

Even my faithful old car was against me!

I wanted to go back to the comfortable church, not here!

Since I was already in the church parking lot, I reached over to pick up a new box of tissues laying on the seat of the car and resigned myself to giving this place one more try.

The compelling force in my life had begun, a force so strong and so powerful that *nothing* was to stand in the way of total commitment. The compelling force that drove me was a desire to see that I knew everything there was to know about this man Jesus Christ, and a desire to see that everyone knew Him personally even as I thought I did. However, even though I had met Him casually, I had not met Him personally.

I started going to church every Sunday morning and was so spiritually charged up – but completely miserable during the altar call week after week – that it seemed to me my soul was absolutely torn out of my body.

I begged...I pleaded...I cried...Sunday after Sunday, and said, "God, You know I want to be a totally dedicated Christian – what's the matter with YOU? Why don't you take ALL of me?" You see, I knew something was not right in my life, but I didn't know what it was.

This went on Sunday after Sunday for months and months. I couldn't wait to go to church, and I couldn't wait to get home afterwards because I was so torn up inside, and because I never took along enough Kleenex to wipe my tears. The Bible says, *"You must be born again."* How stupid can some of us be? Over and over again I asked God what was the matter with HIM.

By Thanksgiving of 1965, God had restored my left eye to 20/20 vision with the help of a contact and glasses, and I went to church very grateful for what He had done for me. As I sat there and listened to the sermon about thanking the Lord for what He had done for us, God continued to deal sternly with me, but only because of His great love and because the Holy Spirit was really working on me to show me the way.

Seeing Myself

When the sermon was over, I didn't dare look down because I was afraid to! I knew I didn't have a stitch of clothes on! Do you know what it's like to be sitting in church absolutely naked? It's horrible. God had stripped me of my outer clothing to show me exactly what I was, and all I could say was,

"What's the matter with YOU, God, you know I want to be dedicated 100 percent" – and I wasn't even born again!

Just about this time a young man named Ed Waxer from Campus Crusade for Christ came into my office and gave me a little booklet entitled The Four Spiritual Laws. I read this with extreme interest and thought, "Is that all you have to do to be born again?" And I decided, "This is really easy."

I was so excited with that little book because it made being born again so wonderfully simple that when I went home that night I put my children to bed early and even though I lived in Florida and it was a hot sultry night, I jumped under the blanket with a little flash light, turned it on and read the little booklet, because I didn't want anyone to know what I was doing. The first thing it says is, "Jesus, forgive my sins." I stopped there and said, "But Jesus you know I haven't sinned." I thought sin was something BIG like murder.

Then I kept reading. "I open the door to my heart and I invite you to come in." I waited. I was expecting a big boom, a clap of thunder, lightning, fireworks or an explosion of some type, but nothing happened!

A thought entered my mind, "I must have opened the door the wrong way." I said, "Jesus, I'm sorry I opened the door from the right side when it must open from the left. I beg your pardon. I open the door to my heart on the left side and I invite you to come in." Immediately I said, "You didn't come in."

Then I thought, "It must be an overhead door." I said, "If it's an overhead door I open it and I invite you to come in." Then I added, "You didn't do it!"

Every night I repeated this process. I wore out more batteries than you could believe!

And nothing happened!

When I went to church the next Sunday morning I was determined after asking Jesus to come into my heart all week, describing doors of glass, crystal, precious jewels, colors and everything else, I knew He hadn't come in (because I kept saying, "But you know I haven't sinned"). I went to church this particular Sunday morning and made a fervent statement with every ounce of my being crying out to God. "I am not coming out of this church until **I know that I know that I know that Jesus Christ is living in my heart.**"

That Sunday I could not wait for them to sing *Just As I Am*. But they didn't sing it! They sang, "*Have Thine Own Way, Lord. Have Thine Own Way.*" I thought the pastor was a traitor. While we were singing that song, God reminded me of sin in my life. And in the loving, wonderful way that God has, He nudged me and said, "Remember the penny you stole from your mother when you were four years old?" That was 45 years before! "God, how did You know about that?"

Then He reminded me of another sin that wasn't quite so nice. Horrified, I said, "You knew about that, too?" Then my whole life flashed before me as God spoke to me in that special precious moment and said loving but firm words that I will never forget. He said, "I know every rotten thing you've ever said!" I knew God had ears, so that didn't surprise me.

"I know every rotten thing you've ever done." I

knew God had eyes, so that didn't surprise me.

"I even know every rotten thought you've ever had." **Then I knew that God knew,** and I cried out, "God have mercy on me a sinner."

I honestly believe this was a greater shock to me than discovering I wasn't a Christian. Suddenly Frances Gardner crumbled into nothing and died to self and was born again, because for the first time I said, "Oh, God, what's the matter with ME?"

Then I added another statement. I said, "God, if You want what's left of this mess, You take me but You take all of me because I want nothing of myself left!"

Then, being a business woman, I made a deal with God. There are many people who don't think you can make deals with God but I stand as living proof that you can. I said to Him, "God, I'll make a deal with You. I'll give you *all* of me (wasn't that generous?) in exchange for *all* of You." We made that deal and I got the best end of it!

Someone had asked me once when I was "saved."

I had answered, "Saved from what?" Finally I realized that I had been saved from sin, a thing I had refused to admit that I had ever committed, even though the Bible says, *"ALL have sinned and fall short of the glory of God."* It also says, *"The wages of sin is death."* I had been spiritually dead all these years because I *could not admit that I had sinned.*

And *only then,* because I had finally received God's forgiveness for my sins, could I ask Jesus to live His life through me, and be the Lord of my life. At last I understood what the "Lord" meant.

But, interestingly enough, when salvation came, it came so quietly I don't even know the date.

No lightning.

No thunder.

Just peace and calm.

Chapter 2
Just As I Am

After church, I went home thinking of nothing but Jesus. I had stopped at every store which was open and tried to beat Jesus into everyone. I didn't want to think about anything else. I didn't want to think about my printing company, my business, my friends, my house. I was so totally out of this "world" that it was unbelievable. For the first time in my life I realized that God loved me. When God wrote in my Bible, "Frances Gardner, I love you" it was the first time I was aware that God knew I existed as a person. Now, I was saved and I just basked in the love of God. I could just feel God's arms around me. A 10,000 pound weight had been taken off my shoulders.

I went to bed and the peace of God flooded my soul. Suddenly I began to cry. I cried and cried and cried just as if I was broken hearted! I kept thinking to myself, "Why am I crying? I'm happy!"

I couldn't stop.

The next night, the same thing happened. I cried and cried and cried. My pillow would be soaking wet. I thought of everything in my life I had done wrong! I told God over and over again that I was sorry for everything I had ever done and I promised I would never do it again! Not just saying, "I'm sorry," but turning away from it. That is true repentance! Instead of tears of sadness, I felt such joy and relief that I cried tears of happiness. I cried every night for more than two months! "God tears" washed me; He washed all the desire to sin out of my life.

The euphoria I felt after finally being "saved" lasted two glorious days. I floated around the printing company all day long. The third day I was running from one press to another and when I looked down at my chest I could both see and feel my heart beating. I thought I would explode!

I said, "Jesus, You're in there! That's not my heart-beat! That's the heartbeat of Jesus Christ!" Right there in the middle of all those sinners who worked in my printing company, I said, "Jesus, I shut the door to my heart. I lock it. I throw away the key. Now You can't ever get out of there!" After all I had been through, I was never going to let Him go!

As a baby Christian, I thought I had discovered the greatest thing in the world! The freedom I felt, the joy, the excitement were indescribable. I wanted to tell everyone in the whole world about Jesus and how He had miraculously saved me from my sins. I was quickly labeled a "fanatic" as I drove up and down the street, stopping at every opportunity to share with everyone who would listen. I thought, "There's no one talking about Jesus! I've got to go out and win the whole world to Jesus!"

What Happens Next?

I wonder how many people have felt the call to

come to Jesus as the famous song "Just As I Am" was being sung? One of the most misunderstood phases of Christianity is the state of our being when we accept Jesus Christ. Having worked with many as they were led to Jesus in various ways, probably the biggest single reason given for not wanting to accept Christ at a particular time is, "I've got to get rid of some bad habits first."

Oh, foolish sinner, God wants each and every one of us "just as we are." Even though my Christian experience does not span many years, it spans a lot of people, and I have never yet met one who by himself "got rid of some bad habits."

The most amazing thing about Christianity is that there is only one thing a human has to do, and that is to surrender or yield his life totally to Jesus. Of course, this is the most difficult thing in the world to do, and something many people fail to accomplish.

In this particular phase of my life, I believe God dealt very kindly with me. In most things I had to put up a fight and struggle, but I was so stupid I really didn't think there was anything wrong with any phase of my life now that I was a Christian.

Even though I had denied all the sin in my life, sin had certainly been there. **I smoked five packages of cigarettes a day.** Lighted cigarettes and/or cigarette butts lay all around in the ashtrays in my office, in my house and in my car. I drank martinis like they were going out of style and I swore like a trooper. I never said four consecutive words without a swear word coming out. But the day I was born again, God cleaned up my mouth. Since that moment, no swear word has ever crossed my lips. No dirty joke has ever entered my mind. I had been the life of every cocktail party because I knew more dirty jokes than anybody else. After meeting Jesus, I couldn't remember a dirty joke if my life depended on it.

God cleaned up my mouth.

God cleaned up my mind.

"Therefore if anyone is in Christ, he is a new creation: old things have passed away; Behold all things have become new" (II Corinthians 5:17).

"And do not be conformed to this world but be transformed by the renewing of your mind" (Rom. 12:2).

I didn't have the same old mind that I had as a sinner. I had a brand new mind! I couldn't swear. I couldn't think of dirty jokes again. I couldn't even listen to them because He cleaned up my ears – my ears used to love to hear all that kind of dirty talk. From the day I was saved I could not listen to anything that was even close to being filthy.

However, God didn't get rid of all my bad habits immediately. I've heard some people get miraculously saved, cleaned up and delivered all at once. It took longer for me.

My daughter was a teenager and I enjoyed working with young people. I began working with the youth in the church. They were in and out of my home constantly. I always drank my nightly martini and smoked incessantly in front of all of them because I felt there was nothing wrong with either activity. Nobody had ever told me there was anything wrong with smoking. I was still smoking five packages a day – one cigarette after the other from morning to night.

As the days went on, a verse in the Bible kept coming to my mind: *"I beseech you therefore, brethren, by the mercies of God, that you present your bodies a living sacrifice, holy, acceptable to God, which is your reasonable service" (Romans 12:1).*

But, I couldn't quit smoking. I was smoking four cartons a week. I couldn't even buy them all at the same store because the employees would comment, "You just bought a carton." I was truly a "cigarette-holic." I made all kinds of excuses as to why I was out of cigarettes so quickly, always adding, "I don't really smoke that many!"

Suddenly, I began to feel uncomfortable smoking in front of my pastor. Even though he had never once commented on my smoking, I discovered I could no longer keep chain-smoking when he came into the office. Finally I couldn't even continue smoking the lighted cigarette in front of him. I had to let it burn itself out.

One night as I was working late, he stopped at my office with the next week's bulletin for printing. I had just bought a new carton of cigarettes and had opened the first pack. I had just lit the first cigarette when he walked into the room. I had an urge to eat it, lit end and all, so he wouldn't see me smoking. However, since he had caught me red-handed, I quickly said, "I'd quit this stinking habit if I could!"

He didn't give me a lecture at all. He just pointed

a finger to heaven and said quietly, "Why don't you ask Him to help you?"

Surprised, I replied, "For a little thing like cigarettes?"

He said, "A little thing like cigarettes."

I continued, "A stinking little thing like cigarettes?"

"A stinking little thing like cigarettes!" he said.

"You've got to be kidding!" I thought God only handled the big things, like earthquakes or hurricanes. I didn't know He cared about little things.

The pastor left me sitting in my office, holding the cigarette and watching the smoke as it curled up to the ceiling. When the smoke got high enough, I got my eyes on God and I cried out, "God, I'm a mess. You know I can't quit. But if I'm not presenting my body a living sacrifice, holy and acceptable unto you" (because that was the verse I had read that morning before I left for work), "take away the desire."

With that, I put my hand down and I put the cigarette out.

You'll be glad to know that I have never smoked another cigarette nor have I ever had a desire to smoke since that time!

Because I knew it was finished, I took a little piece of paper, wrote the date on it and put it on top of the package of cigarettes and sealed it with scotch tape. At three o'clock in the morning when I finished working, I went by my pastor's house and threw the cigarettes up on his porch. When he came out the next morning, he said, "I knew who it was and I knew exactly what happened!"

After the births of both of my children, I had tried to quit smoking. Each time, I broke out in a horrible skin rash. I itched all over and scratched continuously. I spent many thousands of dollars on skin problems. The rash disappeared both times after I started smoking again so I gave up trying to quit smoking. Suddenly **in a split second, the cigarettes were out of my life forever!** And I didn't break out in a rash, either!

Peer pressure was turned on. Talking about Jesus and/or God was not popular. I remember my daddy saying up until the day he died, "We don't discuss religion or politics in this house. That's a personal thing. You just never discuss it with anyone."

As hard as it was for me to stop smoking before salvation, it was harder for me to be quiet about Jesus and what He had done for me after I was "born again." I shared my excitement with everyone whether they wanted to hear or not. Some were quite patient with me. "You'll get over this." "I'll give you a couple of months. You'll be back to the parties again." "We've seen others go through this same thing. You'll soon see this is just a fad."

An uncomfortable feeling began to happen to me when I would drink my favorite martinis. I loved martinis. I loved the dry taste. I never put the vermouth in them because I just liked the gin straight. Gin and olives, that was all I thought was in a martini. Oh, how I loved the gin and the olives at the bottom. They were so good! I never thought there was anything wrong with drinking. People used to always say, "Drink a little wine for your stomach's sake." Since it was a quotation from the Bible, I thought drinking was very acceptable.

I certainly wasn't an alcoholic, although each time I drank a little more than the last time to feel good. The "high" that I would get after drinking a few of those delicious drinks was great. Or so I thought! After a short time with Jesus in my heart and reading God's Word, I found myself going much higher on God than I ever went on martinis.

My girlfriend was an alcoholic. She certainly didn't plan on being one, but she would drink one after another. As her saturation level was reached, she needed more and more and more. I thought if I drank with her, maybe she'd quit. I still never thought there was anything wrong with drinking.

God was dealing with me. Man could have talked his head off and I would never have listened. Since I was having so much fun as a Christian, I realized the world of alcohol was not a real world at all. It was a fake, a poor imitation of life. God's world was the real one and that's where I wanted to be – where I wanted to stay.

Nobody really talked about Jesus very much in those days! Most people didn't know who He was even though they often used His name in vain! I got so excited about what had happened to me, I had to tell everybody. Jesus really opened my mouth and I haven't shut it since, and I don't intend to!

I was never shy or timid before I got saved. I didn't suddenly become shy or timid afterwards either. I used every opportunity to share my excitement. Everywhere

I went, I talked – the cleaners, the grocery store, the gasoline station. Some people noticed the difference in my behavior and would ask what caused the change. I gladly told them in great detail about my new exciting life.

My family thought I had gone crazy. My son, Tom, came in one day and said bluntly, "Mother, you're going to curl up into a fuzzy ball and blow over in a corner and die if you don't quit all this church stuff. You're not any fun any more. You used to tell dirty jokes. You used to smoke and drink. Now, you don't do anything that's fun any more."

I said gently, "Honey, but I'm really living now. I'm really living!"

Not too long after that, I overheard somebody talking with my daughter, Joan. "What's the matter with your mother? She's acting so strange these days."

Joan replied, "Mother's going through the change of life" as I entered the room.

"That's right. That's right, I'm going through a change of life," I interjected, "but a different kind of change of life than any of you are thinking about. When Jesus came into my heart, He really changed my whole life."

One evening, I visited my girl friend. Her husband thought I had flipped my wig and become a "religious fanatic." He made a martini, set it on the counter in front of me, looked me straight in the eye and insisted, "Well, holy Josephine, you have probably gotten so holy and pious that you won't take a drink any more."

How do you tell your old friends that you "don't drink any more?"

I looked at that drink. The most amazing thought came into my mind, "I don't want it. I really don't want it. Even just yesterday, I loved that dry taste of a martini. Now, I don't want it at all."

I didn't know what to do. I felt like I was backed into a corner and didn't have the courage to fight. Probably because I was still partly a spiritual chicken, I cried out again for God to do something for me.

I looked up to God quickly and thought, "Oh God, what do I do? Do I pick it up and drink it to be sociable?"

I didn't want it!

The Holy Spirit had done a cleansing job on me and I didn't want to touch that drink. I also didn't want to offend my host.

"Should I pick it up and hold it? No, that's compromise and **God never honors compromise!**"

The Bible had become my one and only reading material. I remembered Paul saying, *"I am not ashamed of the gospel"* (Romans 1:16). I closed my eyes just for a moment. I was desperate. When I looked back at that martini glass, *God had changed it into a snake,* the sign of evil in the Bible! And the Person who had changed my life so drastically had made another change only because I had yielded my all to Him.

God spoke to me as loudly and clearly as I have ever heard anything, *"Alcohol has no part in your life."*

I had to make a choice. Do I please God or do I

please man?

I looked at my host and very calmly said for the first time in my life, "No, thank you. I don't drink!"

Instantly, the snake changed back into a martini!

The world had put the pressure on.

God took the pressure off.

No one has ever offered me a martini since that night! Somehow they knew without my ever saying anything that I just didn't drink any more. I didn't HAVE to drink because I had only to remember and recall the presence of God to be lifted up to the highest plane, and how could anyone ever be downhearted or sad when in His presence?

When the Christmas season came the first year after my conversion, many of my friends did not invite me to the usual Christmas parties because I "had really changed." By the second year they were beginning to realize this was not a temporary thing, but that something had really happened in my life. Many of my friends joined in the same walk, and many watched my life in amazement, but could not enter the same narrow gate. However, they invited me to their parties the second year with the reminder, "We'll have Coke for you," or, "You can drink your eggnog plain."

I didn't enjoy going to cocktail parties any more because the conversation was so inane and so shallow, so I went only on rare occasions. And it amazed me to see what happened. Suddenly everyone was asking me questions, and the highball glasses were sitting on the tables and the drinks were going flat because the ice cubes were melting in them.

A friend took a picture behind my back at a party one night and it was real interesting...the only person with a glass in their hand was me! And the expressions on their faces as they listened to my testimony told a very interesting story.

Looking For Kicks

I think people who drink are looking for "kicks" and are trying to get themselves on a higher plane than they are during an average day, and so they resort to the artificial stimulation of alcohol to give them "kicks." If only they realized the truth of Ephesians 5:18: *"And do not be drunk with wine, in which is dissipation; but be filled with the Spirit,"* they would find that a spiritual "kick" is a permanent state of being – a way of life, if you please – that replaces any and all of the worldly things in a heavenly manner.

My heart cries out daily because of those who are so blind they cannot see the life that wins. Even though they are amazed at the change which has come because I asked Jesus to live His life through me, they realize that the changes were made because He was willing to accept me "Just As I Am," and today the story is turned around because they, too, accept me "Just As I Am." But what a difference in the two meanings! As the wonderful words of Paul say in Philippians 1:21: *"For to me, to live is Christ, and to die is gain."* By dying to self I have really learned to live.

And no one ever asks me to smoke a cigarette or drink a martini any more.

Just one month after I met Jesus, my 13-year-old daughter, Joan, accepted Jesus. Several months later, we were talking about the changes in our lives. I turned to her and asked, "What made you turn to God so quickly and accept Jesus just one month after Momma did?"

She simply replied, "Because of the *change* I saw in you!"

Chapter 3

I Find The Holy Spirit

"However, when He, the Spirit of truth, has come, He will guide you into all truth..." (John 16:13).

"...but be filled with the Spirit" (Ephesians 5:18).

"If we live in the Spirit, let us also walk in the Spirit" (Galatians 5:25).

It's a marvelous thing that God doesn't reveal all of His kingdom to us at one time – I doubt if we could stand it in one big dose. Maybe that is why He gives us only a little glimpse of truth at a time, because each tiny glimpse is so overwhelming and so overpowering that a massive dose might be fatal.

Once the compelling force in my life had begun, everything in my life was pointed in one direction only – all I could think of was Jesus Christ, the love of my life! Everything else fell by the wayside and was completely secondary to this Man who had changed my entire being – my entire way of life – my entire way of thinking – my entire reason for living!

But I still had such a long way to go – and I still do. And then one day I was setting some type for a job which mentioned a desire to be filled with the "Holy Spirit."

My pastor always seemed to drop by the office just when some spiritual crisis arises or does the Lord send him there? I couldn't possibly imagine what being filled with the Holy Spirit meant, so when he came in to pick up some work, I just asked him point blank, "What does it mean to be filled with the Holy Spirit?" And I hope in reading this you will remember that most of my life I had gone to church and Sunday school, but I had never heard of the power of the Holy Spirit.

He said, "When you are born again and God forgives your sins, you become a clean vessel which the Holy Spirit can fill with power for your Christian life." This made no sense to me, and I wondered for a minute if he was kidding me. I couldn't understand what in the world the Holy Spirit was.

Then I did what I always do when I discover something new in Christianity. I ran for the Bible and looked up every reference to the Holy Spirit. I went to the Bible store and bought every little tract and book which I could find concerning the Holy Spirit. Also, about this time our Bible Study Class began studying the Holy Spirit, and I discovered that in Ephesians we are commanded to be filled with the Holy Spirit.

It's amazing what happens to your life when the Holy Spirit comes in. He brings a power unbelievable to a non-believer.

The "King" Of Christianity

The ability to witness and to transmit the fact of God's love is there – the ability to win others to Jesus becomes a reality – the ability to follow God's will becomes a routine thing. In other words, the Holy Spirit is the "zing" of Christianity.

Each time I have sat down to write on this book I have asked God to fill me afresh with His Holy Spirit, and I have asked the Holy Spirit to use my brains and my fingers on the typewriter to bring this story to life so that anyone who might read it will feel the vibrant living thing that Christianity is. A personal relationship with Jesus Christ is the only thing in the world that's worthwhile, for the Bible says: *"Seek ye first the kingdom of God" (KJV)*.

As I read that recently I wondered what comes second. I have never found time to do anything but *"seek ye first,"* because the seeking and the searching is a lifetime vocation to me at any rate, and I doubt if there will ever be time to seek anything else.

Not only that, the Bible says the fruit of the Spirit is love, joy, peace, patience, kindness, goodness, faithfulness, gentleness, self-control. When you are filled with the Holy Spirit, you have ALL this (and heaven, too), and with all the wonderful blessings of His Holy Spirit, how could you possibly want for anything except more of the wonderful promises of God?

A Special Quality

There is a special quality to those who are filled with the Holy Spirit. He imparts a special vibrance, a special "come-alive" warmth to an individual, a special radiance, a special outgoing Christian love which is distinguishable in a room, on a street, on a stage, or anywhere an individual happens to be. The defeated Christians today – and there are many, many of them because they do not ask to be filled with the Holy Spirit.

The Holy Spirit gives freedom from the things of the world... the Holy Spirit brings every single part of you, both physical and mental, into an exciting relationship with Jesus Christ! Without the Holy Spirit you will fail.

If you want to be a failure in Christianity, don't ask to be filled with the Holy Spirit. If you want to be an automobile that runs out of gas and can never run again, don't ask for a refilling of the Holy Spirit. If you want to lead a useless life, don't ask to be filled with the Holy Spirit.

BUT if you want ACTION in your life, ask right now to be filled with the Holy Spirit. And get the debris out of the road, because action is what you'll get!

Chapter 4

I Learn To Pray...In The Bathtub

"And all things, whatever you ask in prayer, believing, you will receive" (Matthew 21:22).

Once the "bug" of Christianity had really bitten me, I couldn't read enough, study enough, buy enough inspirational books, pray enough, or accomplish enough of anything I wanted to do.

Unable To Pray

The biggest stumbling block in my Christian life, however, seemed to be my inability to pray out loud. I could send up all kinds of prayers to God in silence, by just thinking, but I discovered I just couldn't open my mouth and pray out loud.

At my age it's difficult to admit you don't know how to pray, but I do remember telling my pastor if he ever called on me to say a public prayer he wouldn't get a prayer, but a big "thud" which would be me fainting dead away.

I went to a study group on prayer and found myself learning how to pray to God, in the name of Jesus Christ, and by His Holy Spirit, and after what must have been months, I finally was called on to say a benediction. My throat tightened up, my heart pounded so loudly I knew everyone could hear it, and if I had opened my eyes I know I could have seen it beating. I finally struggled through a magnificent prayer which consisted of three words, "Thank You, Lord."

And then I cried.

I went home that night and wondered why I couldn't pray, and then I felt that I had really let God down. The wonderful God of love who answers prayers, the God who had never let me down, and I couldn't even talk to Him out loud!

After I got home that night I asked God to teach me how to pray. I asked Him to fill me so full of His Holy Spirit that I would be just running over with prayer. And I got into the bathtub. Something about the soothing quality of water (or bubble bath) made me decide this was the perfect place to learn how to pray and, anyway, nobody could hear me.

I have prayed more prayers in my bathtub than probably any other single place. The quietness and the fact that my family never disturbs me makes the bathtub a perfect place to pray.

For the next six months I was probably the most scrubbed, bathed woman in Florida. As I discovered how to pray, a new dimension came into my life, and not only did I discover how to pray, I discovered how wonderful it is to pray, and how easy it is to pray and keep in constant communion with our heavenly Father.

There is one thing I would like to caution the reader about, however, in connection with learning to pray in the bathtub.

In my energetic urge for Christianity, and the surge for maturity, the Lord decided to use me as a soul winner. I had no problem witnessing about what Jesus could do in a life because of what He had done in mine, and because I always asked the Lord to fill me with His Holy Spirit and to speak through me, many individuals have been led to Jesus. But I discovered that when they accepted Christ, the next step was to ask them to pray a prayer of repentance, and I couldn't help because the only place I could pray was in the bathtub!

I often wondered what some new Christian would have thought if I had said, "Would you mind jumping into the bathtub because that's the only place I can pray?"

I never did, though, and I finally did learn how to pray publicly.

Prayer Times

There are many kinds of prayer times. There is the time when it's just "time to pray." I'm not real crazy about this kind because I like to pray when I feel like praying...either because I feel very strongly on some subject or because of some tremendous need in my own life or the life of another.

My children always ask me to say the blessing at the supper table because they know that's when they get to find out about all the fabulous things that happened during the day, and as a result our house has the most unusual "grace" period imaginable. Actually, this is our devotional time because it's the only time we are all together, and this is when we bare our hearts and our innermost thoughts. The prayers that have been answered as the result of this are unbelievable.

Once in a while we do remember to ask that the food bless our bodies as we present them a living sacrifice, holy, and acceptable to God. Dinners have become cold upon occasion when everyone felt led to pray, but I have never had a complaint about a cold dinner caused by warm prayers!

Probably the greatest miracle in my life occurred because of prayer – not just lukewarm prayer, but fervent prayer – but this is a separate story in itself.

Learning how to talk to God can be a fabulous experience, if you will let it. And talking to God can make your entire life fabulous.

I have a little prayer which I send up to God every morning when I wake up, but let me caution you – *don't say it unless you mean it!* Before I open my eyes in the morning I say, "Well, Lord, what fabulous things are we going to do today?"

And do you know what? Every day is *fabulous!* Last Thanksgiving I went to Clearwater, Florida, to be a counselor at the state youth convention and by the time I returned, I was exhausted. We had a death in our church, had a special guest at the morning service, and went to a church dedication service that afternoon, so I was completely ground down. On Monday morning I said, "God, do You think we could have a dumb, dull, stupid day because I'm so tired?"

And do you know what?

I had a real dumb, dull, stupid day! But by Tuesday morning there I was back again saying, "What fabulous things are we going to do today?"

I would like to challenge each of you who read these pages to ask God what fabulous thing He's going to do with you today.

But remember, if you don't have the courage to accept His fabulous offerings, don't pray.

Chapter 5

I Am Baptized

I was "sprinkled" when I was a little girl. I don't even remember exactly when it was nor can I find the baptismal certificate, but during the many years I wore my tarnished halo as a bonafide "counterfeit Christian," I **knew** that I had been "baptized."

After my personal encounter with Jesus Christ, one day in church came the announcement that all those who had been "saved" would be baptized by request in four weeks, and then we heard a sermon on "Why Baptism by Immersion."

For some reason or other, from my early childhood on I remember having an aversion to denominations that believed in "dunking" people. I put this in the same category as the word "saved," and I definitely shied away from anything that sounded like immersion. However, the Holy Spirit took care of this problem for me beautifully, and again God dealt relentlessly but lovingly with me because of my own stubbornness.

Something put doubt into my mind as to whether I had actually been baptized or not. I read all the Scriptural references I could find, and nothing seemed to satisfy me. I talked to my pastor, assuring him that I had been baptized, and he laid the decision right back in my lap. Kindly and gently, but firmly, he said, "You'll have to make your own decision, Frances." I decided right then that he should be more positive about things like this so that he could tell people whether they should be rebaptized or not. But how smart he was...he knew the decision had to be my very own, and not something someone talked me into doing.

I was real busy lining up all my spiritual children for the big event, but in the back of my own mind was the ever present thought of my own baptism.

Our church didn't have a baptismal pool and since I lived in Florida where many people had swimming pools, the baptizing was often done in such pools. I couldn't help but feel this was the living end to put on an old white choir robe and walk into a friend's pool and get your hairdo ruined when I *knew* I had been baptized many years ago. And, anyway, I was forty-nine years old, and it's ridiculous to be baptized with a bunch of teenagers when you're that old.

My pastor came by the office and I said to him, "I have a swimming pool, so why should I go to somebody else's? Wouldn't you like to come over to my house some night **after dark** and baptize me in my own pool?" I thought this was a very simple way not to publicly be baptized. My pastor looked me right in the eye and he said, "No."

That was all he said.

But God continued to deal with me, and I could think of nothing else. I kept thinking I heard the words over and over, "You've got too much pride to be baptized, haven't you?" And again I talked and talked to God, trying to talk Him out of being baptized publicly at my age.

But it doesn't pay to argue with God. I always win when I do, but I only win because I give in to Him. With me the only way an argument with God can possibly end is for Him to have His way in my life.

I finally went to my minister and announced I wanted to be baptized along with my daughter because I knew where I was going, and while I didn't feel the Bible said anything about failure to be baptized keeping you from eternal life, I wasn't going to take any chances. When I sat in his office after church one night and told him this, I felt a thousand-pound weight had been removed from my chest.

The Sunday came when we were all to be baptized, and we were to be at the swimming pool for a public service at three o'clock that afternoon. A number of the teens were over at my house; as we dressed for the service, I felt the presence of God so strongly I knew I had obeyed Him with my decision to be baptized.

I felt I would burst – my heart actually seemed to beat as though it would break out of my chest. I tried to remain calm because some people have emotional reactions to certain things, and others don't, and I don't feel the degree of your Christianity depends on the emotional feelings you have. I knew that no one noticed anything unusual about the way I felt until one of the boys said, "How come you have your dress on backwards?"

I had put on my bathing suit and slipped a shift

over it, and in my utter calm I had put the dress on backwards.

It was a short drive to the swimming pool and when we arrived I was shocked to find such a large crowd there. The minister walked into the pool and one by one baptized the young people. I have a vague recollection of being next to the last, or last, I'm not sure which because something really happened to me that day.

A man in our congregation led me into the water (a problem with my second eye had started and was getting very serious, so seeing was a real problem for me). I remember stretching out my hand to reach the minister because I couldn't see anything without my glasses on –and I don't remember anything else. There is a very vague recollection of him asking me if I had accepted Jesus Christ as my Savior and Lord, and I think I said, "You *know* I have."

I must have been immersed, but I don't remember it except that I was soaking wet; he must have called out my name, but I didn't hear it; he must have walked me to the steps because I couldn't see to walk by myself; someone must have helped me from the pool, but I don't remember anything except the rushing of waters over my face. Before they closed over me, my soul went right straight into the ever-loving outstretched arms of God.

It seems to me we sang "Thank You, Lord, for *saving* my soul," but it was all hazy. My usual talkative self had been awed and silenced by the overpowering presence of God. I couldn't wait to get away

– all I wanted to do was go home and read my Bible. I felt I would scream if anyone talked to me because I didn't want to ever break the spell of the presence of God. I went home, grabbed my Bible, and with the arms of God wrapped tightly around me, I read His wonderful words all afternoon.

I think baptism is the thing that sealed me and bound me forever.

Chapter 6

I Learn To Witness

When Jesus came into my life, He opened my mouth, and I haven't shut it since! And I don't intend to. I had the most burning desire to share what had happened to me with everyone I met, and the Lord who always honors a sincere heart crossed my path with another of the "men in my life."

One day a young man walked into my office and when I looked up from my desk at him to ask him if I could help him, all I could see were the eyes of Jesus looking at me from a different face than I expected. I quickly decided that Christianity had gotten the best of me, and I was really imagining things, until he opened his mouth and said, "I'm Ed Waxer of the Campus Crusade for Christ."

Somehow in the way we never question, God's Holy Spirit had told me here was a brother in Christ, before I ever knew who he was. I am a debtor of Ed Waxer, a Christian of Jewish background, for the time he has taken to help me mature as a Christian.

As I look back on it now, he must have thought I was a batty old lady, but he realized that the drive and the compelling force which possessed me was a dedication to Jesus Christ. I nagged and nagged and pleaded and begged, "Please teach me how to 're-cruit.'" What I really meant was "Teach me how to lead others to Jesus," but in my unchristian jargon I didn't know what to call it except recruiting for God's army. Poor Ed was so busy trying to activate the campus program in the Miami area, he really didn't have time, but finally he promised he would come over to my house and teach me how to "recruit."

I was almost hysterical. He had told me I could invite three other people from the church, but somehow I invited seven, and I made the eighth person. Ed brought another staff member of Campus Crusade and we divided into two groups to learn how to "recruit."

Four Spiritual Laws

Ed showed us how they present the "Four Spiritual Laws" which the Campus Crusade for Christ uses internationally. This is a simplified presentation of the plan of salvation. Ed carefully explained every step and assured us it would work and turn our church upside down if we would try it.

I had been literally dragging people to church with me because I had read that Paul said, *"I have become all things to all men, that I might by all means save some"* (I Corinthians 9:22). I felt that everyone in the whole city of Miami simply had to go to church and hear the claims of Jesus Christ, but to win someone to Jesus...that was something else.

I studied the Four Spiritual Laws and read and re-read them. Our church formed a "GO" Committee. During a meeting the minister gave out "GO" cards or calls we were to make and present the Four Spiritual Laws.

A church friend and I (we were known as the GO-GO girls) made a promise to God that before the week was over we would go and make a call and present the Four Spiritual Laws.

Monday came and I called and said, "Barb, I'm so busy at the office I've got to work tonight. Can we call it off tonight?"

Barb said that was all right with her, we would go the next night. The next night she called me with some phony excuse...And the next night was the midweek service, so neither of us had to make up a phony excuse...Then the next night I called her and gave her a phony excuse. And on Friday she called me because she was having company...And we both decided Saturday would be a bad time to go.

AND SUDDENLY IT WAS SUNDAY! And we had promised God we would make a call before the "GO" meeting at 6:00 P.M. on Sunday. After church on Sunday morning, I called Barb and said, "We pledged – and we just *have* to do it. And she agreed.

Well, I tried to think of everything to make us so late we couldn't possibly make a "GO" call on anyone because I was SCARED. I had temporarily forgotten the Bible says: *"But you shall receive power when the Holy Spirit has come upon you; and you shall be witnesses to Me in Jerusalem, and in all Judea and Samaria, and to the end of the earth"* (Acts 1: 8).

Time Was Running Out

I picked Barb up at five o'clock, and we knew that time was running out, but even so we remembered a friend in the hospital who maybe we ought to go see. But after a hurried conference, we *didn't,* because we had made a covenant with God, and we knew we had to keep it.

We went to the house assigned to us and I did some of the fastest praying in my life – but some of the most stupid. I prayed: "Dear God, please don't let anyone be home. We just can't do this. Please...please." As we got closer I pleaded, begged, cried, rebelled, and asked Him to see that no one was home.

And then I saw a light in the house.

...And then I saw that the door was open.

I reminded God that maybe she was out and had just left the door open and could I please turn around? Relentlessly, God said, "GO."

Both Barb and I nearly fainted when a woman came to the door. We had previously decided that Barb was going to read the Four Spiritual Laws because she had been a Christian longer than I had; so we walked in and I honestly have no idea what we said, but before long Barb was reading the Four Spiritual Laws.

Four very simple, but beautiful laws, all backed up with the proper Scripture.

No. 1 merely states that God loves you and has a plan for your life.

(I won't argue with that.)

No. 2 states that "all have sinned and come short of the glory of God."

(I won't argue with that.)

No. 3 states that "Jesus Christ is God's only provision for man's sin.

(I won't argue with that.)

No. 4 states: "Behold, I stand at the door and knock. If anyone hears my voice and opens the door, I will come in to him."

(I won't argue with that either.)

And then you ask the person you've been talking to if he (or she) would like to invite Jesus to come into their life.

Barb asked the woman if she would like to invite Jesus into her life. And she said, "Yes."

Barb and I both felt as though we had been struck by lightning!

We had kept our covenant with God, but had forgotten that He would be with us, so we were not prepared for success. Oh, how pathetic it is when we don't put faith in God's promises.

Barb looked at me, and I looked at her, and we both thought, "She's kidding." So Barb asked her again and when she said, "Yes" again, we looked at each other and in the same instant we realized how little was our faith. God has never let me down, but I often wonder how many times I have let Him down.

We came to our senses then, and Barb said the only thing either of us could think of to say: "Let's pray." She did, and we felt the presence of the Holy Spirit as He is always felt when someone is led to Jesus.

We said our "good-byes" with tears in our eyes because this had been a tremendous experience for all of us. As we went down to the car, we thanked our

Lord for His tender, loving care which had directed two sincere women who didn't know what they were doing, but knew what they wanted to do.

We flew back to the church and practically tore our pastor apart because we were so excited because we had led our first person to Jesus. We followed this up two nights later with another thrilling win for Jesus, and I did the talking that time.

Since then the Lord has blessed Barb and me many times, but I often wonder if any convert will ever do for us what the first one did.

Chapter 7

I Find Witnessing Is Exciting

There is no thrill in the world which compares with leading someone to Jesus! What happens in your own life when you have "faced" a person with Jesus Christ and he has accepted Him is indescribable.

Do let me give you the only hint I can concerning witnessing: Don't ever try to do it on your own, or you'll fail! As Barb and I went on "GO" calls, we never talked in the car, but prayed, and asked God to fill us with His Holy Spirit and let the words that were to come from our lips be His words, and not ours. Only when you are yielded to His Holy Spirit can you be an effective witness.

Our young people wanted to learn how to win others to Jesus, so one night after a midweek service we held a training class. The pastor was called out, so he asked me to take over and show the young people how to present the Four Spiritual Laws.

I presented them as I would in anyone's home, and as I got to the fourth law concerning Christ's invitation, I realized I was talking to a group made up of about 50 percent non-Christians. I stormed the gates of heaven with prayer asking God's guidance, because how could these young people be successfully taught to be soul winners when they were not Christians?

God's very presence was in the room that night as He touched the young people one by one and they opened the doors of their hearts to invite Jesus in. And I felt my "cup run over" because my physical daughter was now also my spiritual daughter, for she, too, accepted Jesus.

On The Beach

The young people wanted to win others to Christ after seeing a film entitled "Bal Week" which showed Campus Crusaders witnessing on the beaches. Two carloads of us went to a local beach one Sunday afternoon; the young people knew they could really turn Miami upside down by holding an evangelistic movement on the beaches. Barb and I went and sat down to await results and give them spiritual encouragement.

Satan always comes in when he feels Christians maturing, so he planted F-E-A-R into them. About ten youth walked around the beach where hundreds of people were sitting; then they came back and reported, "There isn't anyone we can witness to."

Once the witnessing bug has bitten you, it is impossible to keep still, and I was really champing at the bit. I could see potential in every group singing, swimming, swinging, or what have you; so they said, "All right, *you* do it if you think it's so easy."

I had better explain to the reader right now that I am not a movie star type. In the first place my age is against me for purposes of beauty (but for enjoyment of life, it's really *with* me!). In the second place I

70

would say I'm approximately twice the size of the average woman, so this doesn't add to my physical charms. (It's a blessing, though, when people want to cry on your shoulder to have a big enough shoulder to cry on!) But God made me and He loves me, and so this must be the way He wants me. Who am I to complain?

It's essential when in Rome to do as Romans do, so before leaving home I put on a bathing suit, carefully covering it with a shift. I kicked off my shoes and walked across the sand to the first group I saw.

And what a group! They all were nineteen to twenty-two years old. Real beatniks! Beards, bikinis, liquor, the whole bit. I said, "Lord, you'd better handle this all the way or I'm sunk."

I walked up, sat down between two of the young men, and said, "Would you good-looking young men mind if an old lady sits down with you?"

I hope you will remember that I have been in business for ten years and most people consider me successful, reliable, dependable, and so forth. And the answer of this beatnik group could have knocked me off my feet had I not asked God to do the job for me.

"What are you, some kind of a fruit?" I remembered the old saying, "If you can't beat 'em, join 'em." So I said, "Yes, and if you don't believe it, you can ask my twenty-year-old son. But he'll tell you I'm a square pushed out, or a cube, which is even worse...Now, boys, do we talk your language, or mine?"

Silence.

I told them I was taking a religious survey and would appreciate their answering some questions. They agreed to answer the questions, but they had decided to roast me like a pig on a spit.

I asked them a few introductory questions about their plans for the future, and their nondescript answers indicated that they were all going to be bums. They had no plan for their lives. I said I thought this was fabulous, because since they had no plan, I knew they'd be interested in knowing that God had a plan for them.

One finally admitted that he was going to be a surfer and he really perked up when I told him I was personally acquainted with the world's greatest surfer. "Jesus Christ," I said, "because he didn't need a surfboard; he just walked on the water."

This made an impression on them, and they promptly asked me to go to an Ale House with them.

I declined.

Next, I asked them whom they knew the most about Mohammed, Buddha, or Jesus Christ. They all got real smart-alecky and answered, "Mohammed. Doesn't everybody?" One thing to remember during a survey – don't reply to or comment on any answer regardless of your personal feelings.

At this point I gave a little testimony of my own life and one young fellow said, "Put me down for Jesus Christ, Ma'am."

The Holy Spirit had come to walk on the beach.

I had been sitting there wondering what I was doing on the beach when I hate the sand, the salt, the water, the breeze, and so on. Then I remembered how Jesus witnessed on the shores of Galilee, and I decided if it was good enough for Him, it was certainly good enough for me. And anyway, if He was living His life through me, who was sitting on the beach?

The transition question had been answered, so I asked them how a person becomes a Christian. At this point three others joined the group, so I now had seven. The newcomers joined not because of a personal invitation from me, but because the original four grabbed them into the group.

Their answers would have broken your heart!

"I was born a Christian."

"My parents are Christian, that makes me a Christian."

"Just go to church and you're a Christian."

"It's something about feeling guilty about something or other. I don't know what you have to feel guilty about, but it's something or other, and if you feel guilty, you're a Christian."

"If you go around with Christians – it's something about fellowship that makes you a Christian."

"If you behave and lead a good life, you're a Christian."

Not one of the young persons sitting there knew how to become a Christian. Not one had ever been told that he must be "born again."

Not one knew about accepting Jesus Christ as Savior and Lord.

Not one knew that sinners have to be forgiven of their sins!

In a world where communication is present in all forms: radio, TV, telephone, newspapers, magazines, it broke my heart to realize that none of these young people had ever heard the communication of Jesus.

About this time the lifeguard came up and was going to arrest me for "selling" on the beach without a license. I told him I wasn't selling anything. I was giving it away. One of the young men who originally had intended to roast *me* on a spit jumped up and said: "Take your hands off of her – she's telling us the most interesting things about the Bible we've ever heard."

The lifeguard unhanded me, and I whispered a prayer of thanksgiving to God.

I continued and the stillness of the beach was a surprising thing. I looked up and about twenty people were now listening. My cry went up to heaven as I said, "You do it, Lord, because I don't really know what I'm doing."

And the Lord of my life, as always, came through. I read the Four Spiritual Laws and eight young people nodded their heads in an acceptance prayer and a prayer of forgiveness.

I didn't drive back home after that – I just "floated home on a cloud."

In A Hospital Room

One of the most thrilling conversions I ever witnessed occurred in a hospital room.

I had been asked to call on a man who was seriously ill in the hospital, and when I asked for information so I wouldn't go "blundering in," my pastor said, "Sometimes blundering is a blessing." I said, "Thanks a lot," little realizing the wisdom he had used.

Miami often has severe rainstorms and this was during the rainy season. That particular night it rained over eight inches. The highways were flooded; it took me twenty minutes to get from my office to a location which normally would take me three minutes. The water was completely over the highway, and it was pouring so hard it was impossible to see.

My night vision is not good, so I don't drive often at night. I wondered if the Lord wanted me to turn around and go back home to my nice, dry, warm house, and I asked Him. I heard nothing, so I said, "Well, if You want me to go, You'll have to help me drive this car, and please, please prepare his heart for me as I make this long drive." Again I had asked God's Holy Spirit to go with me.

It took me two hours to drive what normally would have taken thirty minutes, and when I finally reached the hospital and parked the car, I stepped out into water nearly up to my knees. It was almost like a hurricane. I was soaked before I got two feet from the car.

My clothes stuck to me like glue (and I'm too fat to be good-looking in glued clothes), my shoes were ruined, my hair was dripping down in my face, and I'm sure I looked as far removed from an "Ambassador of Christ" as anyone could. I shivered as I entered the air-conditioned hospital (no wonder, I had accidentally gone into the morgue!), but after regrouping myself, I finally found the right room.

Three other men were in the ward, and as I talked a silence fell over the whole room. It was a thrilling moment because the Holy Spirit completely filled the room. Talking to the patient, I realized that God had prepared his heart and that he wanted Jesus in his life. So I merely looked at him and said, "Would you like to accept Jesus right now?" And then we prayed; first I prayed, and then for the first time in his life he prayed and asked God to forgive him for a lifetime of sins.

"Blundering was a blessing" in this case. Afterwards I was informed that this man had sneered at anyone who dared to mention Jesus Christ in his presence, but with God preparing his heart, my blundering was a blessing!

Even In Church

One of my greatest delights after winning someone to Jesus is to watch that person grow and mature as a Christian. The Lord blessed whatever ministry I have by allowing me to be instrumental in leading my best friend to Jesus.

In my B.C. (before Christ) days and D.L. (during liquor) days I spent a lot of time "martini-ing" with a couple whom I enjoyed very much. Shortly after meeting them, I became aware of the fact that for the tiny little person that she was, the wife could consume more alcohol than any person I had ever seen. And somehow or other she never showed the effects of one martini or ten. She never got drunk, or very seldom got drunk in the accepted sense of the word, but I often wondered how she could consume what she did without getting sick, or passing out, or something.

Her alcohol problem became increasingly worse over the years and I tried to caution her (as we drank martinis together) that she should cut down because it just wasn't good for her to drink so much. She's a very beautiful woman, with gorgeous, big brown eyes, and I warned her that if she continued to drink the way she was, it wouldn't be long before she wouldn't be pretty any more, but this didn't seem to faze her. She went deeper and deeper into the bottle.

One time my friend's husband asked me to see what I could do about her alcohol problem because he had to go out of town for several weeks. I decided I would drink right with her, and then get her to stop before she was blotto! I failed to consider my own low tolerance for alcohol, and so before the week was out, she was still going strong, but I was completely baggy eyed and hung over. Then I decided to keep her so busy while her husband was away that she wouldn't have time to drink. Little did I know that after an evening of taking our children places, she would go home and spend the rest of the night drinking alone.

And then I found Jesus! And when you first find Jesus and your friends are not on that road, your friendship remains the same for a short while, but then the love for Jesus overpowers everything else in your life and you discover you don't have anything in common with non-Christians.

Only once on the Christian road did I ever consider looking back. And that was for this friend. But when you really discover Jesus Christ, nothing is worth looking back for, and momentarily I regretted the fact that I had to leave her back there because I couldn't look back. There was only one way for me to go, and I knew it!

She continued to drink, and as she continued to drink, she watched the amazing change that was occurring in my life. She began to call me in the middle of the night and with a tiny little voice crying, "Help me, Frances, you've got to help me." I have talked for hours on the telephone trying to get her to leave the bottle alone, at anywhere from midnight to four o'clock in the morning.

She was attending a church half-heartedly where the gospel is apparently not preached, but in her groping for something she started the search which was to take her where she is today! She was intrigued with the way I was reading the Bible, so she dusted hers off, and started reading, too. But she only read in hers what she wanted to read. We have spent many hours on the midnight telephone discussing our different interpretations of the Bible.

The bottle became bigger and BIGGER and my heart really ached for her. I yearned to have her find the loving arms of Jesus Christ who could protect her from all harm. I had a reluctance to invite her to church with me, so I only went into ecstasy over what each Sunday did for me, hoping to make the claims of Christ sound so appealing that she would want to come with me one Sunday.

And then it happened! One Sunday morning a little

tiny hung-over voice called me and said, "Aren't you ever going to invite me to your church?" I could have cried! So I said, "Come today," and she said, "If I can pull myself together in time, I'll be there."

I went to Sunday school and didn't learn a thing that morning. All I did was pray! I prayed first that she would get there. Then I prayed that the minister would preach the kind of a sermon that would "grab" her, and then I prayed that God would open her heart so that she, too, could have the "abundant life."

God answered all of my prayers.

She got there all right! But she smelled so strong of whiskey she almost knocked me over. She apparently had had a "crying" jag because she showed the effects of weeping.

Second, my pastor must have preached just the right kind of sermon – or did God just use him in the right way?

Third, God cracked open the door of her heart. As in Sunday school, I didn't hear a word of the sermon, because I prayed the whole sermon through.

She returned the next Sunday after crawling in the bottle all week, only this time she didn't smell of alcohol.

She continued coming every Sunday and conversations concerning Jesus became everyday occurrences, but the bottle became a bigger and bigger problem.

My pastor and I had prayed for her so much, because we saw a really lost soul, and because I loved her so much.

And then we had an evangelist for a week's revival

at the church.

If anyone had told me two years prior to this that I would sit in church for eight nights straight, I would have told him he was off his rocker, but there I sat eight nights in a row. I had given my friend a copy of the Four Spiritual Laws to read, and she came to several of the revival services. I could see that she was getting closer and closer to accepting Jesus, and then one night during the invitation hymn, my pastor stepped down from his usual place in the pulpit. This put the three of us in a line – he was on one side of the room, she was in the middle, and I was on the other side. Somehow in that room she got caught in a crossfire of prayer between the pastor and me, and she turned to me and said, "Can't I be a Christian without accepting Jesus?" I said, "Well, not hardly." She cut me off and said, "Oh, well, it doesn't make any difference," and stepped forward to accept Jesus.

Being an emotional woman, I cried, because here was something I had prayed about for so long. She was now my sister in Christ.

I'm not going to tell you that all of her problems ended that night. Maturing as a Christian is sometimes a slow, tedious process. And I think God often tests us to prove our desires.

The alcohol still continued to be a problem, and she tried to quit several times. Finally alcohol ceased to be a problem because it ceased to *be,* but this happened only after she finally yielded herself completely to Jesus.

It is interesting how it finally happened. She had

been invited to a cocktail party and didn't want to go because as she said, "You know I'm weak...They'll offer me a drink and I'll take it, and when I take one, there I go again!"

I said, "When they offer you a drink, say 'No, thank you, I don't drink,' and before anyone can say a word, really get some prayers up to God asking Him to back you up."

She has never touched another drop!

Today she is one of the strongest Christians I am privileged to know. And our Christian love is far greater than our "martini" love ever was.

Many people have asked me why I have such thrilling experiences as a Christian. If you haven't guessed the answer by now, let me tell you it's only because I allow Him to use me, and He will use YOU, too, if you will only let Him.

Chapter 8

My Spiritual Brainchild Is Born

One of the burdens the Lord laid upon my heart early in my Christian experience was young people. As I watch the teenagers of today with boys looking like girls and girls looking like boys, and all of them going down the sin path as fast as their feet can carry them, my heart cries out to help them.

A year or so ago I developed such a concern for young people who do not really know Jesus in a personal way that I asked God to show me the way to make Jesus a reality and a way of life to them. I looked at my own life and realized how much could have been accomplished had I had Jesus on the throne of my life years ago. And I realized the waste of all those years.

I had seen a sign on a billboard which said, "I found how to get the most out of life after most of life was gone," and it slapped me right across the face as a true, but cutting statement about my own life. I thought of the old round of cocktail parties, dances, cigarettes, martinis, the desire to learn the latest dance steps. Recently I was horrified to read in a scrapbook that I had led in an exhibition of the "twist" at a radio broadcast.

So I began to pray.

And I prayed.

And I prayed.

And I prayed.

The summer came and was almost over when I made probably the greatest statement I've ever made in my life. I told my pastor he'd better start ducking. He knew I had been praying that God would show me the way to take Christianity to the kids in high school; he also knows when you ask God for a big request like that you'd better start ducking if you don't mean it, because He will really give it to you. I knew that God would give me the answer before school started, and so I knew there wasn't much time to back out if I didn't really mean it.

I prayed even harder.

One day a customer who is a wonderful Christian came into my office and I mentioned my prayers to him. Because the hand of God has human fingers many times, he picked up the telephone, made a call, and put me in contact with a man who has the same burden for young people that I do.

The net result of this was a frantic meeting (he drove some fifty miles to get to my house for a rush meeting, for the church youth camp started the next day). We almost talked the whole night through as we shared our ideas, and from this exciting meeting Alpha/Omega was born.

Alpha/Omega

Alpha/Omega was to be a Christian youth movement to win others to Jesus and to show them a wonderful "way of life." It was decided to take Alpha/

Omega off the ground with a "Blast Off" program designed to appeal to young people. Because of this, I met two more of the "men in my life."

A big, good-looking football player from the University of Miami named Rick Strawbridge had been voted "the least likely to succeed on the Christian Road" a few months prior, but those who gave him this award had not reckoned how God was working in his life and how great was his decision and his dedication. Rick came into the office one day with Ed Waxer, and thus began another of the great loves in my life.

I asked Rick to give the story of his encounter with Jesus Christ at the Blast Off, and in the following weeks my admiration and love for another Christian grew. I learned how to establish rapport with teenagers through the willingness of this young man to share unselfishly of his time. Rick has been one of the strong arms of Alpha/Omega as it has floundered and then grown. So many young people have the idea that religion is for old "fuddy-duddies," and Rick really brought sparkle into it with his **"P.T.L."** (Praise the Lord). Few young people will ever come out and say, "Praise the Lord," but we hear "P.T.L." said all the time.

At the beginning of the year a drama trio from Anderson College had performed at our church in a play called "The People Vs. Christ." A young man named Fred Clemens did an outstanding job of acting in this most unusual play. I got a chance to know him because I asked the trio to stay at my home. The next day I was giving a barbecue so the young people in the church could get a chance to know them and see these wonderful living examples of Christianity. This would prove that Christians really do lead the most exciting lives in the world.

We had such an exciting evening we forgot to go to bed. We were sharing all the fabulous Christian experiences we had all had, and at four-thirty in the morning I started the barbecue sauce for the party later that day. I'll never know how we made it to church on time, but we did! When I saw my pastor I flatly announced that I had a "Christianity hangover" from overindulgence. I will say this – I have had hangovers in my time, but this was the only one I ever enjoyed. And I have also spent many boring evenings in the most elegant of cocktail lounges, country clubs, and other places, but I have never spent a boring evening discussing Jesus Christ.

Now that I look back, it seems to me that most of the conversation centered on the word "saved." This word went against my grain from the word go and I guess it still does. I spent most of the night trying to convince Fred that it was much more acceptable and loving to ask someone to accept Jesus instead of asking him to be "saved." During the twenty-four hour period Fred spent at my house, I discovered what a wonderful Christian he is, and what a wonderful sense of humor he has.

So when the time came to think about who to use in the "Blast Off" for Alpha/Omega, his name came to me. I wrote to him and asked him if he would do a comedy act poking fun at the unchristian acts of today's teenagers. Since Fred was studying for the ministry, he was floored by my request and wrote that he would pray about it. In the final analysis I guess I outprayed him, for he came and did an outstanding and never-to-be-forgotten job.

The girl in the play was a charming young lady named Linda Cotton, and since I had lost her address, when I wrote Fred asking him to do the acting bit, I asked him if Linda would come along to sing.

Fred wrote back that Linda has a brother named Gene who he felt was really great and since they were going to be staying at my house, it would be easier for two fellows to stay than a fellow and a girl. So on blind faith I accepted Gene Cotton, another of the great loves of my life. Fred told me Gene was entertaining the troops in Vietnam, but would be back in time for the show.

Frantic preparations went on as we readied for the big show because I sure didn't know what I was doing – I had never been involved in anything like this.

The days grew closer and then one day the phone rang and it was Gene Cotton. He was in Atlanta changing planes and he would arrive in Miami two hours later.

I called my pastor and asked him to go with me because suddenly I panicked. I thought: What if I don't like him?...Can I be *sure* he's a Christian? What if he's a lousy singer and what kind of a guitar player is he?

We drove to the airport, the flight arrived, and we waited while it unloaded. This was really "guitar players" day. About the first passenger off the plane was carrying a guitar (or a machine gun case) and my heart sank! Here was a bearded beatnik of the first degree.

I was afraid to look at him, so I died a thousand deaths before he rushed into the arms of a waiting female beatnik.

I breathed a little easier.

And then I saw another guitar case. This time I really flipped! What was carrying the guitar case would have scared anyone! I really prayed!

And the second guitar went by.

I decided I wasn't going to look any more because I couldn't stand the strain. I would wait until someone asked me who I was.

Then the last guitar player came off the plane.

And the Lord had introduced me to a brother in Christ who was to greatly influence my life, because we shared the same compelling drive in our miles apart, years-apart, altogether different types of lives. But because of our mutual desire to show young people "His way of life," Gene Cotton and I joined hands in Alpha/Omega.

Folk Singing

From the very first meeting with Gene Cotton until the frantic "good-bye" after the Alpha/Omega Rally, the Lord continued to cross my path with this particular brother in Christ. Little did we realize at that time how the hand of God was working in bringing the abilities of two Christians together to further His kingdom.

When Gene accepted Christ, he rewrote the words of a familiar folk song entitled "I Can't Help But Wonder Where I'm Bound," changing it to "I No Longer Wonder Where I'm Bound." I have his permission to share his song in this book because it truly tells the story of all Christians.

And I can't help but wonder where I'm bound, where I'm bound,
No, I can't help but wonder where I'm bound.
Well, once I led a life that was toil, sin, and strife,
Never thought that I would see the day
That I could look down without having to turn around, But it's here, my Lord, and I know it's going to stay.
And I no longer wonder where I'm bound, where I'm bound,
No, I no longer wonder where I'm bound.

'Twas a life of sin and woe, and I hated to let it go,
But I heard a voice come calling from above,
"If you'll but follow me, I'll give you life eternally,"
So I gave myself for everlasting love.
And I no longer wonder where I'm bound, where I'm bound, No, I no longer wonder where I'm bound.

Now I've started on my way, and I live by Him each day, And I know in Him I always will abide.

And when I meet that Chosen One,
He'll say my job has been well done-
"Won't you come with me and sit down by my
side?"
And I no longer wonder where I'm bound, where
I'm bound, No, I no longer wonder where I'm
bound.

For me, life began at the cross of Calvary and the old road ended there, too.

One of the most unusual answers to prayers came as a result of my friendship with Gene and I always refer to this incident as "The Night the Lord Used a Cherry Pie."

During Gene's initial visit to Miami, I made a real gooey whipped-cream cherry pie. Gene immediately generated a very special "love" for this particular pie and on his subsequent visits to Miami I made one each night. During a phone call on my birthday he asked me if I thought I could make a pie and send it to him in Columbus, his hometown. I said "Sure." He said, "You're kidding. How could you get it to Columbus?"

My only comment was, "I'll make the pie; you ask the Lord to get it to you." We ended our conversation with my telling him the pie would be in Columbus two days later.

I flew to the store (I hope you will note I never walk, I always "fly") the next day and bought the ingredients and two metal pie tins to ship the pie in, and then I prayed. I said, "Lord, to strengthen the bonds of Christian love between my brother in Christ

90

and me, will You please see that this pie gets to Columbus tomorrow?" (I hope you will note that I did not ask the Lord to get it there because I made the best cherry pie in the world, or because Gene liked the cherry pie, *but only to strengthen the bonds of Christian love.*)

And God answered that prayer. I picked up the telephone and called an acquaintance of mine who is a pilot and said, "Bob, I've got to get a whipped-cream cherry pie to Columbus tomorrow. Do you know anyone who flies the Columbus run?"

Now everyone calls up utter strangers, don't they, and asks them to fly a pie someplace or another for them? I asked as nonchalantly as if I were asking him to tell me what time it was, and he replied the same way – just as if it were a very ordinary everyday experience to fly whipped-cream pies – and said he didn't know anyone who flew the Columbus run.

BUT HE HADN'T RECKONED THAT GOD WAS WORKING IN THIS SITUATION! He called me back within a few minutes and said, "Frances, you'll never believe it, but the regular pilot on the Columbus run is sick, and my best friend has the run. Take the pie down there at four-thirty in the afternoon to his house and he'll be glad to take it for you." I just said "Thank You, Lord," took the pie down to the pilot's house, called Gene and told him to meet Pie Flight No. 304 arriving in Columbus at 9:05 and ask for the pie being carried special delivery. Gene later told me they really were looking for him at the Columbus airport when he picked up the pie because apparently some people just don't understand that it's possible for the Lord to charter a 727 jet to fly a pie someplace for the sole purpose of strengthening bonds of Christian love. I'd like to give a special thanks to Eastern Airlines for unknowingly cooperating with the Lord.

Chapter 9
The Real Meaning Of Christmas

Christmas, 1966, became very special in my life, because it completed my first full year of being a Christian. Each year I had sent out a "Christmas" letter to all my friends, telling them of the events of the year: how many kittens the cat had, how we fared during the hurricane, and so forth. But Christmas took on a new dimension. I completely rebelled at the thought of sending out the usual "newsy" letter and so instead of the funny, frivolous Christmas letter I usually sent, the Lord laid upon my heart a letter telling what had happened in my own personal life.

And the interesting thing is, when the Lord lays a burden upon you there is no getting away from it (and neither is there any desire to get away from it), and so a *real* Christmas letter was written and sent to all my Christian and non-Christian friends. Even my Christian friends suggested that I should not send it because it was so definite in its meaning. They said, "People will think you're nuts." I said, "Great!" The following Christmas letter was the result.

1966
THIS WAS THE YEAR OF OUR LORD

Each year we always have so much to
tell, but this year we have a different
message to bring,
The usual things happened...and the
unusual happened.

I guess it really started last year when I
had my eye operation. Looking back
now, I realize this was probably the
biggest blessing that ever happened to
me, because it caused me to open my
spiritual eyes and look things over.
Much to my amazement, even though I
had been brought up in church, I
discovered that I really did not
personally know Jesus Christ.

And then I met Him. . .and nothing
changed. . .except my whole life.

My Bible which had been covered with
dust for years, became the most
interesting book in the entire
world...and a thirst was created for
knowledge which I hope is never
satisfied.

There's a verse in John which says: "I
am come that they might have life, and
might have it more abundantly." How
true! I always thought my life had been
very exciting, but never have I

experienced such a fabulous life, and as new doors open, I look forward to each day with anticipation,

And to tell you about the excitement day by day would take pages, so I'll sum it up and say, "This was truly THE YEAR OF OUR LORD."

To many of you who have read my Christmas letters for years, this one may seem strange. I hope you understand because my wish for you is the

    PEACE,

        JOY, and

            HAPPINESS

which fills your life when you know Him personally.

        Frances

My family continues to be fine. Tom bought a new house this month. Joan continues to be the delight she has always been.

Never have I ever sent anything which had the impact of this simple message. Many people called to tell me it had made them stop and look at their own "Christianity" or "Churchianity" as some of them called it. Some wanted to know how they, too, could know Jesus Christ in a personal way.

...And my life was changed forever.

Chapter 10

God's Plan For My Life

As I write this final chapter of the now saved "unsaved" Christian, I remember the words in Psalm 46:10: *"Be still, and know that I am God."*

My life has been so enriched and so full since I finally became totally bound to Him that I have often felt I would actually burst right out of my physical self .

There came a plus into my life the day that Jesus first reigned supreme, and that "plus" has been there ever since. For one brief fleeting moment I wondered if it was worth losing my friends for, but the moment was so fleeting I hardly remember any more that it ever existed. And the plus sign in my life is the cross of Jesus Christ.

I publicly announced on my fiftieth birthday that I had hardly been able to wait for the fabulous fifties. Because my fiftieth year was really my first complete "year of our Lord" it was the most fabulous year of my life. I recently saw my fifty-first birthday and Alpha/Omega surprised me with an unbelievable birthday party. I expect my fifty-first year to be even more fabulous than my fiftieth...And just wait until I hit the spiritual sixties!

Christianity is a state of being – a way of life! And if I have painted the abundant life in glowing terms, I meant to, because there's nothing that compares with it. As I mentioned previously, the biggest sin in the world today is the sin of doubt or unbelief. And this is the sin which keeps many from living the abundant life.

Don't mess around with Jesus if you don't mean it, because He doesn't want just a part of you. The Lord of my life is really selfish – He isn't satisfied with just part of me – He wants all of me, just like He wants *all* of you. And it's a funny thing – **once you have tasted Jesus Christ, nothing else satisfies.** I'll guarantee you, if you really step out on faith the first time, try as you may, you will never be able to go back, because Jesus won't "mess around with you." When he takes you completely and positively because you yield yourself to Him, He brands you with a brand that burns to the very core of your being.

The abundant life gives me a life that allows me to rise above every crisis that may come along in the "worldly world" because *"I am in the world, but not of the world."* Only those who actually experience this can ever understand.

Christianity and the abundant life are not a series of mountains and valleys to me – rather they form a plateau which allows me to stay at an even level all the time. And I feel that the more complete and total a person's dedication, the higher the level of his plateau.

If you want to be miserable, give Jesus a *little* slice of your life. Sometimes I feel people are much better off who don't even bother going to church if that's the extent of their Christianity. I remember years ago saying, "I don't want to go to heaven because I want to be where all my friends are." The amazing thing today is I'm sure there are going to be far less people in heaven than any of us imagine because the Bible says, *"Many are called, but few are chosen."* Every person in this wonderful land we live in has the opportunity to hear the words of Jesus. So many are called, but how many of them actually fail to heed the call of Jesus, and therefore cannot be chosen.

I do not know yet what God wants out of my life. I only know that each day I let Him know that I am available for whatever purpose He has for me. And it's a peculiar thing, it doesn't really make any difference what He shows me now that I am waiting on Him, because since I asked Jesus to live His life through me, what I do is inconsequential, but I'm really eager to see what He's going to do!

And to find out, I'm going to keep on saying every morning, "Lord, what fabulous things are we going to do today?"

* * *

When I wrote the "God Is Fabulous," that statement ended the book. But many people wonder what happens after that. Does that tremendous and exhilarating excitement last forever? The answer is, "Yes!"

One of the fabulous things that God did for me was to give me another man in my life. In 1969, while I was reading Matthew 6:33, *"But seek ye first the kingdom of God and His righteousness, and all these things shall be added to you,"* God spoke to me. He said, "Because you have sought Me first, I want to give you a husband to love you and take care of you all the days of your life." Because I put His plans for my life first, God gave me my beloved husband, Charles Hunter. As I always say, "Charles is the most fabulous husband on earth – he spoils me stinking rotten and **I love it!"**

We have lived and written nearly fifty books, have ministered all of the Great Commission (Mark 16:15-18) to multiplied millions all over the world as we have personally preached in nearly fifty nations and probably in every nation through our books, videos and audio tapes.

The next two chapters will help you understand why the joy of the Christian life goes on and on...

Chapter 11

A Marked Woman

The day I was saved became a special day in my life, because I became a marked woman – a woman branded by God – a woman who had an indelible brand burned into me by the fire of God. I am a marked woman because wherever I go that brand goes with me and whatever I do that mark shows on me. **I'm glad I'm a marked woman.**

When I was a very young girl, I saw a movie called **The Mark of Zorro.** I remember the hero of this story was a very swashbuckling sort of individual and he always won every fencing battle in which he had participated. To my knowledge he never lost a battle. When he ended up and had killed his foe or had disabled him or totally put him out of the way, he always ended with a great flourish and made a "Z" on the chest of the man he was fighting or on a nearby door or wall. When they found someone with sword wounds they always knew who it was because Zorro left his mark upon them.

In the natural the man who played the role of Zorro was a very talented man. He was a man who had great ability for fencing and he had a lot of agility with his feet because he could move out of the way quickly when somebody else went to plunge a sword into him.

He was a marked man because of his great ability but he also left his mark.

Any person who is a marked individual is going to be the same way. You're cut out by God and you are going to leave a mark on every person with whom you come in contact.

I'm a marked woman.

I have no choice.

God put His indelible seal upon me years ago.

I love to look in the dictionary especially when I'm going to write a new book or start making a new talk or delving into new subjects. I love it simply because it opens up my mind into many different areas than I have been thinking at that time.

I looked up the word "mark" in the dictionary just to see what it meant. It gives a lot of interesting little descriptions. It says, "To put or make a mark or marks on." When God puts a seal on you, it's done with indelible ink and you cannot get it out.

When you go into a grocery store and you buy meat, many times you will find something purple on the meat and you'll think, "What is this purple stuff on the meat?" They mark meat with grape juice and they put "Choice grade A" or whatever choice it happens to be. Grape juice is not permanent.

Another definition was "to designate or identify by a mark or marks for certain reasons."

Haven't you ever known somebody who just seemed like had everything and could do everything? I've known people who had such an ability, anything that was mechanical they could fix, anything that was electrical they could fix. If you had to put together children's toys, they knew how to put them together. Then there are those of us who can't do anything like that but praise God, *"I can do all things through Christ who strengthens me."*

Many times your abilities will mark you for success. But God doesn't care how many abilities you have or how little ability you have because when He puts His mark on you, **then** you are bound to be a success!

Another definition is "To show plainly, to manifest, to make clear or perceptible such as a sentence like this: Her smile marked her for happiness."

Haven't you seen people who were smiling every time you saw them and they looked happy? Then haven't you seen people who had a very disagreeable look on their face, and every time you looked at them the corners of their mouth were down? Their unhappy look marked them as being unhappy. A person who walks around smiling all the time is a person who is marked for happiness because you can tell that there must be something good happening on the inside of them.

Charles is a perfect example of this! When he was a little boy his coach at school told him, "It takes thirteen times as much energy to frown as it does to smile." Charles made up his mind right then that he was always going to smile so that he didn't have to use thirteen times as much energy. He's gone through life that way. As a matter of fact whenever you see Charles, he's always smiling and I think that's a wonderful characteristic to have because his smile marks him for happiness!

Another definition was, "to distinguish or to set off, to characterize as great scientific discoveries marked the 19th Century."

In the 19th and into the 20th Century we have had some tremendous scientific discoveries. We went to the moon for the first time in the 20th Century. Look at the things that have been invented: radio, television, automobiles, airplanes, computers, air conditioning, MRI's, X-ray machines, ball point pens, microwave, clothes dryers, nuclear weapons and a number of things we take for granted in our daily life. These two centuries have been **marked** with great scientific inventions.

Another definition was, "to put a price tag on something such as merchandise."

When you go to a store, almost everything you buy has a price marked on it. Today when you go to a grocery store, all they have is a funny little bunch of lines which they run over a computer which reads it and it tells you the price.

When you try on a dress or a sweater in the department store there is a price tag on it which tells you what it is and then it will also tell you the cost of it.

God's price tag was Jesus and the cost was His life-blood so you and I might have eternal life.

As I thought about the word "marked" I thought about marking. In other words when you identify something by a particular mark on it, I thought about marking cattle. Cattle owners put their brand on them so that regardless of where the cattle strays out of where their fences are they can still say, "That's mine because that has my brand on it."

I looked up the word "brand." One of the most unusual definitions of this word says, "It was formerly a mark made upon a criminal by burning him with a hot iron, hence it was a stigma or a mark of disgrace."

Years ago if somebody committed a crime and it was not a crime where the punishment was death by hanging, but a misdemeanor or lesser activity, they would brand them on their hand so whenever they put their hand out, there was no way you could miss the fact that this person was a criminal. That kind of a marking was a real disgrace.

But...there is another kind of a mark and this is the kind a mark that I love because I am a marked woman and **nothing can ever change the fact that I am a marked woman.**

Another definition describes what you and I are as marked individuals belonging to Jesus.

It says, "A mark burned into anything by its owner as a means of identification as upon a cask or cattle."

When Charles and I were in Holland we brought home a copper milk can and on it was burned "1857" and the name of the dairy. In other words that mark identified that can as belonging to a particular dairy. It also identified the fact that the dairy was put into service or came into being in 1857. It wouldn't make any difference what you did to that antique milk can, that "1857" and the name of the dairy would show up very, very plainly.

When they took milk from the farms into the dairy there would be many, many milk cans there and to be sure you got your own back, you always marked your cans with your name and probably the year that your dairy started.

It also means, "to impress indelibly as with a brand."

There is a date that is branded in my memory.

The day that is of a special importance to me was February 8, 1966, because that was the day that I became a marked woman. A woman who was branded by God with an indelible branding which will never come off. I can have my skin peeled, I can scrub and scrub, but the brand of God that He put upon me that glorious day will still be there!

Normally when they brand you it's done with fire. That's the way they mark cattle. They will heat a branding iron and where they put it on the animal, they burn that part of their hair off so that their skin shows and you can always see that brand. It doesn't make any difference how long any of the other hair grows, it doesn't make any difference how old the animal gets, that brand is there because it's an everlasting brand upon an animal.

When God marks you, God makes it an indelible marking! All Christians are so marked by God that we should be obvious to the whole world. It should be so simple to look at a Christian and think, "Wow, that person is a Christian." We can never be secret service Christians. We should be so marked by God that the whole world can see exactly what we are, unless we try to cover up the marking.

Saul was marked by God. God is relentless! Once God starts after you, you might as well give up because God's not going to let you go! When God carves you out of a whole herd of cattle or sheep or human beings, He begins to tighten the circle around you (this is what a cowboy on a horse does). He cuts out certain animals from the rest of the herd so they can be marked, and that's exactly what God does to us.

God began to mark Saul. I'm sure that Saul was marked many years before he became aware of the fact that he was a marked man. I have always called the Holy Spirit of God the relentless hound of heaven. When that hound of heaven gets after you He is not ever going to let go. That's what God was to the man who was called Saul and who later became Paul.

In the 7th chapter of Acts Saul told them to go ahead and stone Stephen because Saul was out there killing the Christians and doing everything that he could because he did not like this "new doctrine" of Jesus Christ. He was very vehement about it.

If you have a loved one in your family who is very vehemently against Jesus Christ say, "Praise the Lord", because that means God is having an influence on their life. They wouldn't fight so badly if it didn't mean anything to them. I always look upon these people who are so reluctant to come to the Lord Jesus as individuals like Saul! When God begins to cut you out from the rest of the herd regardless of how far and how fast you have run from God you had better watch out because you are about to get it! You might as well just give in and say, "Here am I Lord."

Saul had just finished saying to go ahead and stone Stephen. Praise the Lord Stephen looked up and said, "Father, forgive him and don't blame them for this." And he died.

The next verse says that Saul was not only consenting to Stephen's death, he was pleased and actually approving. Can you imagine him standing there and saying, "Hit him again. Hit him again. I want to see him dead. I don't want to see him alive." The devil was kicking up his heels because the devil knew that God was going to get Saul and use him powerfully.

Acts chapter 8 says, *"At that time a great persecution arose against the church which was at Jerusalem; and they were all scattered throughout the regions of Judea and Samaria, except the apostles. And devout men carried Stephen to his burial, and made great lamentations over him."*

Stephen was a man who was mightily filled with the Holy Spirit of God. Yet Saul was excited about seeing him killed.

It said, *"As for Saul, he made havoc of the church, entering every house, and dragging off men and women, committing them to prison."*

Can you imagine being so angry and so aggravated that you would go into a house and pull out men, women and children and bring them out to be killed or put into prison because you hated the gospel of Jesus Christ?

I want you think about that person of yours who hasn't received that branding from God, who hasn't gotten that special God mark. They really haven't done anything that bad have they? Have they killed men and women and children just because they hated the gospel so much?

God has His eye on people like that. I'm sure He looked down at Saul and He thought, "Look Saul, why don't you just give up?" Once God begins to cut you out of that herd you might as well give up because you don't really have a chance. (And you shouldn't want one.)

Let's get over into the 9th chapter. *"Then Saul, still breathing threats and murder against the disciples of the Lord, went to the high priest and asked letters from him to the synagogues of Damascus, so that if he found any who were of the Way, whether men or women, he might bring them bound to Jerusalem."*

What an ambition! Can you imagine somebody like that? Can you imagine somebody in your family saying, "I'm going to get a letter out so I can arrest all those Christians. I'm going to bring them with chains and with fetters and throw them in the jail."

Look what happened! Beloved, when God puts His mark on you and when He begins to draw that circle closer and closer and closer, you had better watch out. God is about to do something special.

It says, *"And as he journeyed he came near Damascus, and suddenly a light shone around him from heaven. Then he fell to the ground, and heard a voice saying to him, 'Saul, Saul, why are you persecuting Me?' And he said, 'Who are You, Lord?'"*

That was the Spirit of God convicting him. I believe that Saul suddenly knew that he was a marked man. I believe he knew beyond a shadow of a doubt that he was a marked man because when the Holy Spirit begins to draw that noose tightly around your neck to make you a marked individual you'll know it!

He said, "Who are You, Lord?" Somehow or another he knew that it was Jesus Christ.

"And the Lord said, 'I am Jesus, whom you are persecuting. It is hard for you to kick against the goads.'"

Years ago when sheep were moved from one place to another, the shepherd carried a "goad." It was a stick with a ball on the end which had little porcupine spikes all over it. Every time the sheep would start to get out of line, the shepherd would hit them with this prickly little goad. This really hurt, so the sheep would kick up its heels and get right back in line!

Jesus said to Saul, Why don't you quit kicking at the goad because it's never going to do you any good.

It says, *"So he, trembling and astonished, said, 'Lord, what do You want me to do?' And the Lord said to him, 'Arise and go into the city, and you will be told what you must do.' And the men who journeyed with him stood speechless, hearing a voice but seeing no one. Then Saul arose from the ground, and when his eyes were opened he saw no one. But they led him by the hand and brought him into Damascus. And he was three days without sight, and neither ate nor drank."*

He was really a marked man because it's interesting to note that the very first thing he did was to fast for three days and three nights!

He was a marked man because God had chosen him.

There was another marked man who came on the scene. This might apply to you because it has applied to me many times.

It says, *"Now there was a certain disciple at Damascus named Ananias; and to him the Lord said in a vision, 'Ananias.' And he said, 'Here I am, Lord.' So the Lord said to him, 'Arise and go to the street called Straight, and inquire at the house of Judas for one called Saul of Tarsus, for behold, he is praying. And in a vision he has seen a man named Ananias coming in and putting his hand on him, so that he might receive his sight.'"*

How would you feel if you were Ananias? Remember, Ananias knew who Saul was. He knew that Saul had a habit of going around killing Christians and I'm sure that Ananias didn't want to get killed any more than you and I want to get killed. Here's God saying, "Ananias, go." Ananais was a marked man. He had absolutely no choice because God spoke to him and said, "Go down to that street named Straight."

Then it continues, *"Then Ananias answered, 'Lord, I have heard from many about this man, how much harm he has done to Your saints in Jerusalem. And here he has authority from the chief priests to bind all who call on Your name.'"*

In other words, Ananais was saying, "God, he has a letter in his pocket and that letter tells him that he can kill me. I don't want him to kill me."

"But the Lord said to him, 'Go, for he is a chosen vessel of Mine to bear My name before Gentiles, kings, and the children of Israel. For I will show him how many things he must suffer for My name's sake.' And Ananias went his way and entered the house; and laying his hands on him he said, 'Brother Saul, the Lord Jesus, who appeared to you on the road as you came, has sent me that you may receive your sight and be filled with the Holy Spirit.'"

Two marked men – Saul, a wild, wicked sinner, one who was out killing the Christians, and Ananias, a good Christian man, marked by God to minister to Saul. But God brought down that branding iron and when He put it on Saul, He changed his name to Paul. God said to each of them, **"You are a chosen instrument."**

A marked woman is a chosen instrument. A marked man is a chosen instrument.

I often think about Paul. He said, "I was the worst of all sinners."

I have often said of myself, I was the worst of all the sinners because I think back on what I was before I met Jesus as my Savior and Lord and how I praise Him for His goodness.

A very interesting thing happened to me on February 8, 1966. You may never remember that date but it is important to me because that's the date God took a branding iron and said, "Frances, you are a marked woman. I have put a mark on you that you'll never be able to get away from. I have marked you for my service. I have called you to walk with Me all the days of your life. Frances, don't run. Frances, don't kick against the goads, because you are marked and wherever you go that mark will be upon you."

I'm so glad that I didn't kick at the pricks or kick at the goad. I'm so glad that I surrendered! It took a long time for me to settle on the exact date, but I finally did.

I've been a fanatic since the day I got saved and I personally believe that's the way everybody should be. I believe with my heart and soul that when we are fanatical we become a normal Christian.

I went out of the church that Sunday and stopped at every store that was open and I tried to beat Jesus into every person I met. Something glorious had happened to me and **I wanted everybody to have the same thing that I had!** Do you know why? Because I'm a marked woman. I'm a marked woman because when God put His mark on me He said, "I'll never let you keep your mouth shut about Me. I'll never let you talk about the things of the world. From now on you will talk only of Me." He put a big mark on me. He branded me with the fire of the Holy Spirit because I believe the day I was born again I was born in the fire of God! **I was never born in dead ashes.** When I got up from the altar I was on fire for God and that fire has never gone out! That fire burns more brightly all the time.

After I wrote this first book, God is Fabulous, I remember the first news release which was ever written about me. It's a funny feeling when you're a new author and you've never written anything before. When they told me they wrote a news release about me, I thought, "I wonder what they're going to say. Are they going to say I was born in a log cabin? Are they going to say I only weighed two pounds when I was born?" Many thoughts entered my mind. The news release started out, "Frances Gardner (that was my name then) has had a phoenix experience." Then it went on to tell what a phoenix experience is.

I want to relate this to you because I believe that many of you were marked by God with a phoenix experience and you've never quite let that phoenix experience do what it was supposed to do.

According to mythology, **and I don't believe in mythology,** a phoenix was a huge, huge bird and very, very beautiful. There was never more than one of its kind at a time.

God never made any of us the same. He made each and every one of us different. That's why each and every Christian is totally unique and different in God's sight. With all the billions of faces God has created on this earth, there are no two which are totally identical. There are identical twins and yet there is always a little tiny something that will make you be able to tell them apart. **God is the originator of creativity.** This is why God makes each one of us different. He makes each one of us unique and very special to Him as well.

The phoenix lived a certain span of time on the earth. Then they all did exactly the same thing. When it was time to die, they would fly until they found the very highest mountain they could find and there they would build a nest. The great phoenix, knowing that it had to die, began to flap its wings first slowly and then with a little more energy and a little faster and a little faster. Because the nest was so close to the sun it created such heat that the fanning of it caused the nest to burst into flames and eventually the great bird was totally destroyed in the fire.

The bird was dead and there was nothing left but ashes of the nest and ashes of the bird. There was nothing of the actual bird left because the fire would consume the feathers and everything that was a part of the bird. But **always,** always in the ashes there was a little worm. A little worm that never died. This little worm grew up to be the next phoenix.

That's the way you and I have to be. You and I have to die to self so that Jesus Christ can rise up in us so we will become the creatures in Christ that God wants us to be.

It was interesting that the news release said that Frances was never born in dead ashes. She was born in the fire of God. I remember the verse of Scripture that says, *"For zeal for thy house will consume me"* (Psalm 69:9). I really felt that God was a consuming fire which had consumed everything that was in me and everything that was even not in me, and I became a brand new creature in Christ.

I remember over the years as I have thought back that there were little times in my life when I felt real "religious." I remember when I was married. I had to be married in a church even though I certainly wasn't a regular attender. The only way I can express how I felt at that particular time is I remember I felt a little twinge of religion! It really didn't mean very much to me, but God was sending a rider to cut me out of the herd, until He got me all by myself.

I remember when my first husband died. At his funeral I had a little twinge as I was listening to the words that were said over him. When the doctors told me that he was dying of cancer, there was enough "religion" inside of me that I thought, "I can't let him die of cancer until he joins a church." **Joining a church will never make you a Christian** but at that time I thought he had to join a church. I was insistent because I wanted to make sure that he was a church member before he died. He did join a church and was baptized. When he died, I remember feeling that I had done a good thing.

I remember this little twinge. There was something in there and I didn't even recognize what it was at that time, because sometimes when we are running from God we don't understand these little nudges of the Holy Spirit. I remember thinking, "I wonder what it would be like to be a missionary?" Something within my heart was stirring and I didn't know what it was. Then I looked at my son who was five years old at that time and I thought, "I could never be a missionary because I would have to take him with me and he's too young to go to Africa."

All I could think about was to be a missionary you had to go to darkest Africa wearing a long black dress and carrying a seventy-eight pound Bible and be miserable because all you would do is sit in the middle of the jungle withering and rotting away! I began to look at the things of life that I had liked. I had had five years of tremendous sickness with my husband. I remember it took all the money that I could make and all the money that we had to try to keep him alive.

Suddenly I thought, "I want to make money and have all the clothes and all the things that money can buy." I squashed all of the tugs at my heartstrings and put them to one side.

I was a marked woman. God didn't let me go with that. He let me move to Florida and I remember thinking, "I think I'll join a church because that would be a good place to make friends." I joined a church and got involved in some religious activities there. Every once in a while there would be a nudge in my heart that I didn't quite understand. I wish I had realized that God had marked me, that God had carved me out, that I was branded and I just didn't have enough sense to know it.

When you're marked by God, you cannot get away from Him. I don't care how far you run, how high you go, how low you go, you can never get away from God. I love what David said, *If I go to the highest heights or if I go to the lowest depths I can't get away from You.*

I think it's wonderful when God puts His mark on us. **When God puts His seal upon us there is nothing we can do except become a lover of God.** That's exactly what I am.

I was called for healing when I was first saved. I was called not only to be in a healing ministry but I was called to be healed. The day I got saved, I didn't believe that God still healed today. I had heard about these wild people who had camp meetings and they pretended that people got healed but I never really thought that anybody actually got healed. I had Addison's disease which is terminal. My thyroid was not working at all and my body would not assimilate artificial thyroid and so they were giving me nineteen grains of thyroid a day just to keep me alive and even then I would sit in a chair, fall asleep and fall off of it and sometimes sleep for two or three days at a time.

The day I got saved, when God put His mark on me, I came out of that service totally healed of Addison's disease. Nobody prayed for me. Nobody talked about healing. I wouldn't have believed them anyway if they talked about healing and said that God still heals today. I did not know that in the salvation package is deliverance and healing.

I was so wound up and I was in such a state of euphoria the day afterward that I totally forgot about taking the thyroid and I never thought about it for probably six months and suddenly I thought, "I'm dying with Addison's disease. I haven't taken my thyroid." Then I realized what had happened to me! **God had totally healed me!** I went back to the doctor and my thyroid was absolutely normal and there was not a single solitary sign of the Addison's disease left.

God marked me for healing. As soon as I got saved and began to read the word of God then I discovered that God wanted to heal. **God's will is to heal.** I discovered that Jesus Christ is the same yesterday, today and forever. If He healed yesterday then He is going to heal again today. If He healed again today, then He's going to heal tomorrow and right straight down the line.

I began to lay hands on people. This was before I had the baptism with the Holy Spirit. I have to be real honest with you, my track record wasn't very good because the first one I ever laid hands on died and I was so disappointed, but I had been marked by God and there was no turning back. I was a marked woman and I knew I had to keep on. It didn't make any difference to me if they all died. I would have gone out and found some more people and laid hands on them too.

When you're marked by God it is impossible for you to do other than what God wants you to do. I remember when people came to an altar I would counsel them for their marriage or for spiritual help or financial help or even when they were sick I prayed for them and I believed they were going to get healed. The fact that they didn't get healed didn't phase me one single solitary bit because all I knew was that I was marked and that I had no choice except to do what God called me to do.

One day I went to Bradenton, Florida. I was laying hands on the sick in a non-Pentecostal church and nobody was getting healed. Suddenly a man appeared out of nowhere. To this day I can remember what he looked like and I remember the circumstances perfectly because God branded all of these in my heart. This man walked up to me and without any adieu whatsoever or any introduction he said, "God has given you the gift of healing, why don't you use it?" I thought, "What does he mean?" I didn't really understand what "the gift of healing" was but I remembered that I watched the man as I saw him go and suddenly when he got to he door, "poof" he just disappeared! **Could it have been an angel?** I really think it was. I believe that God sent an angel into my life at that time even though I didn't believe that angels were for today. I believe with my heart and soul that God marked me to have a supernatural experience by having someone say to me that "God has called you into the healing ministry and He has given you a gift of healing."

That's probably why I never gave up even though I prayed for ten thousand people and maybe ten of them got healed and that was all. I never gave up because God had put His mark on me and God said, "I've marked you. You're a marked woman. I have marked you to be in the healing ministry."

I continued to lay hands on the sick and then I came to Texas. When I got saved I said, "I'm so in love with God that I'm going to have a mad, wild love affair with God for the rest of my life." I wasn't the least bit interested in men – God was enough!

I had two children. I had been married and I was widowed and I certainly wasn't interested in getting married again because there was just so much I wanted to do for the kingdom of God. I knew that all a husband would do would be to get in the way. There was no time for marriage, or so I thought.

The men in my church began to pray for me because I was so wild where God was concerned. They said to the pastor, "She needs a husband. She needs a husband to travel with her." At this time I was traveling all over the United States and I would take Joan with me whenever I could get her out of school and she could go with me. If it was vacation time I would take her. But for some reason or another the church began to pray that God would send me a husband. I began to pray against the church. I remember saying to one man, "I'll outpray you."

When Charles gave me an engagement ring, this man came up to me and said, "I guess I outprayed you didn't I ?" He really didn't outpray me because God had marked me out for marriage! Just like God has a special mark on you if you will just wait for the right one.

God marked me out because He had selected a marked man in Houston, Texas. Charles had gone to church all of his life but just a couple of years before I met him, he was carved out of the herd because God saw in him a tremendous response and God reached down, put a big seal upon him and He burned the brand of Jesus Christ right into Charles Hunter.

God marked Charles for marriage. He marked me for marriage. We hadn't even met each other. I came to Houston on a speaking trip where I met Charles. Never saw him again. Never had a date with him. Went back home and never even thought about Charles again, but when God marks you, you're marked! Eighty-eight days later Charles and I were married because God had marked us and He had called us to be married to each other.

God didn't call me to marry just anybody. He called me to marry another fanatic. When you put two fanatics together, you are going to have a wild experience.

God marked us for the baptism with the Holy Spirit. I was a marked woman. I didn't even know it.

I was just like brother Paul. I was kicking against the goads like nobody you ever saw in your entire life where the baptism with the Holy Spirit was concerned. I wouldn't have spoken in tongues for anything because my church taught that it was evil and that it wasn't for this day and time and that it was strictly of the devil!

God is relentless. When God marks you, you might as well give in because Charles and I got caught with the baptism with the Holy Spirit. We were just laughing the other night, remembering how we fought against the baptism but that's because we didn't understand that the Great Commission of the Bible says that those who believe "will speak with new tongues."

The day I got saved I said, "God, I'm going to have to go out and win the whole world by myself because nobody else is talking about Jesus!"

Over in the last chapter of the book of Mark, Jesus said a wonderful and exciting thing. He gave us the Great Commission of the Bible. God said, "I've called upon you, Frances, to be instant in season and out of season to preach the gospel, to heal the sick, to cast out devils, to teach other people and expect them to do exactly the same thing.

"And He said to them, 'Go into all the world and preach the gospel to every creature. He who believes

and is baptized will be saved; but he who does not believe will be condemned.'"

Then Jesus made one of the most tremendous promises. I remember when He said, "I've marked you and you're a marked woman! He didn't just say that to me, He's saying that to you too. He's saying, **You** are marked. He said, "I'm marking you with a sign. And these attesting signs will accompany those who believe."

Jesus said, *"In My name they will cast out demons; they will speak with new tongues;* (The baptism with the Holy Spirit.) *they will take up serpents; and if they drink anything deadly, it will by no means hurt them;"* (That's a sovereign protection of God that gives you power over the devil.)

You're marked and the devil knows it! You're marked because you have more power than the devil. And the last eleven words that the Lord Jesus said were tremendous. He said, *"They will lay hands on the sick, and they will recover."*

The Living Bible says, *"They will lay hands on the sick and heal them."*

"After the Lord had spoken to them, He was received up into heaven, and sat down at the right hand of God. And they went out and preached everywhere, the Lord working with them and confirming the word through the accompanying signs. Amen."

You are marked. What are you marked for? **You are marked for everything that God asks of us in His word.** He says, **"Be ye holy as I am holy."** You are marked for holiness. When God cut me out of the herd of sinners, He said, "Frances, I've marked you to walk in the beauty of My holiness. I've called you to walk in holiness because without holiness no man, no woman, no boy, no girl will see God.

He marked me to walk in total commitment to Him. God marked me to give my whole life. He said, "Frances, I put a seal on you. I've got a brand on you. I've got a mark on you that you can never get away from. Wherever you go around the world, the world is going to see you're a marked woman. Not a mark that you're going to be ashamed of. Not a mark that you're going to hang your head and say, 'I'm a criminal. I shouldn't have done this.' But a mark that you belong to Jesus because you are a marked woman."

I want you to stop right now and make a list of all the things you can think of for which He has marked you. I want you to evaluate yourself and ask yourself, "How plainly do my marks show?"

If you can't figure out the things for which God has marked you, think of the things that I said caused me to be a marked woman. Am I a woman totally different from anybody else? No, because we are all called to be special people! **We are all called to be chosen instruments in the kingdom of God!**

"What Has God Marked Me To Do?"

Has He marked me to be a soul winner?
Has He marked me to be a preacher?
Has He marked me to be in the
    ministry of helps?

Has He marked me to heal the sick?
Has He marked me to cast out devils?
Has He marked me to have the
    compassion of Jesus?
Has He marked me for holy living?
Has He marked me to love the unlovely?
What has He marked you to do?

I remember when I was a little girl, we would buy a little picture book which had little black and white pictures on it. It also had tiny little dots on it, but to make the dots come to life you had to put water on them. Wet them and suddenly the color came out!

Maybe the marking for some of the things that you've been marked for is real faint because you have never put enough of the living water on it.

I want to pray right now for you because God has put a mark upon you. **You are marked by God.** You have been cut out of the herd and you have been selected to be a chosen instrument of God.

"Father, in the name of Jesus I thank you that I'm a marked woman. I thank You, Father, that there is such an indelible mark upon me that there is nothing that I can do to ever get away. Father, regardless of where I go I can never get lost from You because You can always find me wherever I am. I thank You for that. I thank You that I can never be hidden from Your sight. I thank You that I never can be taken out from under Your protection because I keep my eyes on You. Father, I thank You as we evaluate ourselves in this closing prayer that You're going to reveal to each and every one of us where we need to put a little more living water.

"Do we need to put a little more living water on our hands so that we will lay hands upon the sick?

"Do we need to put a little living water on our tongues so we will win more people to Jesus?

"Do we need a little more living water on the love that we have in our lives so that the love within us will be seen by every person we meet? I thank You and I praise You, I love You and I worship You, Father, that You made me a marked woman! Thank You, Father, that Charles is marked. Thank You for the marking that You placed upon every person who reads this book. I give You the praise and I give You the glory that we will show that we will carry that mark, that brand which You have placed upon us all the days of our lives and that we will do it joyfully, excitedly and enthusiastically all the days of our lives. Father, we give You the praise and the glory. Father, a very special thank You from this marked woman."

Chapter 12

Five Little Words

It has been well over thirty years since five little words changed my entire life... *"Frances Gardner, I love you!"* As I reread this electrifying story of how I met Jesus in such a beautiful way, it reminded me of a very interesting fact.

Even though I have been saved well over thirty years I have never backslidden one single moment in word, in thought, or deed. Unfortunately many people have a yo-yo, up and down, up and down Christian walk. Mine has been a straight line which has constantly gone up and yet I discovered so many people do have those spiritually high moments and then horribly low. When they are high, they are high, but when they are low, they are really low.

Most people think that is the normal Christian life. Personally, I think mine is! People have asked me over the years why I have never had a problem in my life with God and with Christianity. They ask, "Haven't you ever had any problems?" Yes, I've had lots of problems, but I have the answer and His name is Jesus. I have never changed my mind that He is the answer regardless of the problem. He is the answer to every problem in life.

There have been so many people who have told me

that when they had these problems they were red hot and then got cold. I began to try to understand what my problem was. I cried out and said, **"God, what's the matter with me that I never have a problem with You?"**

I asked myself, "Why don't I ever question God? Why don't I ever get mad at God?" I have never been disappointed in God. I have never questioned God regardless of the circumstances, nor have I ever gotten mad at God, nor have I ever gotten impatient with Him.

There were times when I really wondered if it was just me thinking that I had never had a problem but I discovered early in my Christian life that there were only two things needed to be successful in Christianity. One was to **do what God told you to do and the second was not to do what He tells you not to do.**

For many years I have felt it is because I made such a total and complete commitment to God the day I got saved. If you remember the chapter about my conversion, I said to God that Sunday morning (the first and only time I have been to an altar), "God, I'll make a deal with You. I'll give You all of me in exchange for all of You." That's what God gave me and that's what God took from me. He took everything that I was, all the cigarettes, all the alcohol, all the swear words, all the dirty jokes, He took all that away from me. **But He gave me all of Himself.** Then you'll remember I said to Him, "If You want what's left of this mess, take her but take **ALL** of me!" I wanted nothing left. Even to this day I remember exactly how I felt the day I became a Christian. I gave everything I was to God. I held nothing back. Most of the time over the years when people have asked me why I've never backslidden, I have always felt that it was because of the total commitment that I made.

I believe this has a lot to do with it because the only part of you that can backslide is the part you have not given to God. That will continue to backslide but what you have given to God will never, never, never backslide.

And I really thought I was the problem until one day when we were riding in a car in California listening to a tape on the Blood Covenant. It was then that the Spirit of God revealed to me the truth of why I've never had a problem.

You will recall when I was in the hospital I saw the finger of God write in the precious blood of Jesus, "Frances Gardner, I love you." Five little words that changed my life forever.

You cannot see your name written in blood and ever be the same again!

I want you to hold that fact very tightly in your memory. It plays a very important role in the next part concerning the blood covenant.

The Blood Covenant was a deal between God and man.

A covenant is a very interesting and unique contract because a covenant always means that two shall be one. Not that two shall be two. But the two shall be one. A covenant always concerns cutting, and a covenant always concerns the blood.

Many people do not understand the seriousness of the blood that Jesus shed for us on the cross.

The 17th chapter of Genesis says, *"When Abram was ninety-nine years old, the Lord appeared to Abram and said to him, I am Almighty God; walk before Me and be blameless. And I will make my covenant between Me and you, and will multiply you exceedingly.*

"I will establish My covenant between Me and you and your descendants after you in their generations for an everlasting covenant, to be God to you and to your descendants after you." He said, "I will make a covenant with you." Abraham made a covenant with God.

A covenant means you and I have a deal with each other. If you have ever been in a partnership with someone, you know that is a deal which you make with somebody else. You agree to do this and in exchange, I agree to do this. And usually you sign a paper to show that you mean it.

However, in olden times, Jewish people made a covenant a totally different way.

Let's pretend that Charles and a young man are two good Jewish men several thousand years ago. The purpose of making a covenant was because one has something you want and you have something that the other one wants.

In the old days you could tell a lot about a person by what they wore. When you were making a deal with somebody you looked over their coat very carefully because their coat told a lot about them.

Their coat would tell you how many children they had, their coat would tell you how much money they had, how much land they owned, how many head of cattle they owned.

So these two men looked at each other. The young man's coat tells us that he is very poor. He doesn't own any cattle, or land, but does he ever have children! He has a whole flock of them!

He needs to feed those children but he doesn't have enough money. He looks at Charles' coat and thinks, "There's an old man who doesn't have any children. But is he ever rich!" He looks at Charles' coat and says, "Wow! I could use what this guy has!"

Now Charles has a problem because he has an old wife, too. And these poor old things, they just creep along and have a hard time walking over all those rocks. They need someone to protect them because there are a lot of thieves in their area. This young man said, "I can bless him because when he and his old wife get into trouble, I can send all my children to help him out."

That's the purpose of a covenant: to help each other. So these two men looked at each other and they decided they want to make a covenant. Each of them has something the other wants. Old Charles and his old wife need some help because the thieves are trying to steal from them. Charles decides they need to get together so the young man's children can protect him and his wife.

Then they make the first step in their covenant. They take off their coats and exchange them. The young man puts on Charles' coat and Charles puts on the young man's coat. What they're saying is, **"All that I am, I give to you.** My money is yours, my land is yours, my cattle are yours, everything I have is yours"...and then the young man says, "All of my children will now protect you from thieves and robbers and anyone who tries to harm you."

The next thing they did was to take off their swords and give them to each other. The young man was saying, "This is my strength and my ability to war. I pledge it all to you, Charles!" And Charles says, "As old as I am, I pledge my ability to fight to you." The covenant was made so that the young man could protect Charles and his old wife. When Charles took off his coat, he was saying, "My money is at your disposal. Everything that you need, I will give to you!"

In those days a covenant was an everlasting covenant.

It was not a temporary thing, it was permanent and forever!

Next they took a goat or a ram, split it right in half and laid it on the ground.

The figure 8 is the sign of infinity because there is no beginning and there is no end. They began to walk **through the blood** in the shape of a figure eight, meaning that this covenant is an everlasting covenant, it is sealed by the blood, and what they are saying at this particular moment is, **"May this happen to me, may I be split right down the middle if I ever break my covenant with you."**

Charles and I made a covenant the night we were married that we would love each other the rest of our lives. And that everything we had we'd give to each other. It didn't make any difference if I got fat. It didn't make any difference if he got bald. **It was an**

everlasting covenant that we never intend to break, because the penalty for breaking a covenant is to be split right down the middle. So these men are saying to each other, "May this happen to me, and more also, if I ever break my covenant with you."

If Charles should break the covenant he made with the young man, **my responsibility as his wife is to kill him** because **the penalty for breaking a covenant is death.** By the same token, every child the young man has and his wife are obligated to kill him if he should break the covenant. This was not something you did casually.

To seal the covenant with each other, each of them cut their wrist until the blood flowed. When the blood flowed, they rubbed their wrists against each other so that Charles' blood mixed with the young man's and the young man's blood mixed with Charles'.

Then they took salt and rubbed it into the wounds because that action made a scar and there was a very definite reason for making a scar. That scar was your identification mark. Anyone seeing you knows you are protected because you have made a covenant.

Then they would exchange names. If the young man's last name was Evans, he would become Mr. Evans-Hunter and Charles would become Charles Hunter-Evans.

Then they would have a communion meal with each other and as they ate the bread they were saying, "All of my body, all of my life is yours." As they drank the juice from the grape, they were saying, "This is my life blood. It belongs to you." **And then their covenant was sealed.**

Each of their wrists now bears a covenant scar for a very good purpose. Suddenly, along comes a very young, energetic robber and he looks at Charles' coat and sees that Charles is a very rich man. He thinks, "I'm going to kill him and get all his money," and as he comes up to attack, **Charles puts his wrist up in the air** and the robber instantly sees the scar! He panics when he sees the scar because he realizes that Charles doesn't stand alone, Charles doesn't stand with just his wife, he has all of the young man's family along with him: his wife, his children, all their cousins, all their brothers, all their nephews and nieces. He's got them all with him. So the enemy runs away just as fast as he can.

The blood covenant works!

In the 22nd chapter of Genesis, after God had made the covenant with Abraham, the Bible says that God put him to the test. He had given him a son in his old age, and then God said, "Take your son up to Mount Moriah, lay him on an altar, and put your knife in him."

This was his only son. He loved him more than life itself. But Abraham loved God more than life. And because he trusted God he was willing to do what God said. He took his son Isaac up on Mount Moriah and gathered the wood. He made the altar and told Isaac to lay down on it. Abraham had enough faith to believe that God would either raise him from the dead or God would do something because of the covenant they had made with each other.

Abraham raises his knife and just as he is ready to plunge it in, an angel says, "Don't do it. Don't do it."

And he said, "Don't lay your hand on him for now I know that you fear God since you have not withheld your son and your only son from Me."

And Abraham looked up and there was a substitute. There was a ram, so he didn't have to kill his son, even if he was willing to sacrifice him.

Two thousand years ago, Jesus died on a cross. God loved you and me enough that He was willing to let His only Son be crucified, and let His precious blood drip down from Calvary for your salvation and mine.

The Blood Covenant God made with us through Jesus is an everlasting covenant. If we really understand how sacred and precious it is, we'll never want to backslide. We'll never want to do the things of the world.

Do you remember the part of the testimony I asked you to hold in your mind because I discovered why I'd never had a problem with God? And why I hope God's never had a problem with me?

When He wrote my name in blood in the South Miami Hospital, what was that?

That was the way the Blood Covenant was presented to me!

The blood covenant is offered to each and every one of us. Maybe not as dramatically as God offered it to me but it is offered to all of us in salvation. He probably thought I had to see it the way I did or I'd never see it. But it was my **response** to the Blood Covenant which has made the difference.

I looked up to God and said, "Give me back my prayer and I promise You this: when I get out of this hospital **I'll spend the rest of my life seeing what I can do for You and not what You can do for me." Beloved, that's the *only* response.** It's not, "I'm going to try Christianity and see if it works." It is your willingness to obey God in everything He says. A willingness to say, "God split me down the middle if I ever break my covenant with You. I give You all of my life in exchange for all of You."

Make that commitment today.